Is a Good God Logically Possible?

James P. Sterba

Is a Good God Logically Possible?

palgrave
macmillan

James P. Sterba
Philosophy
University of Notre Dame
Notre Dame, IN, USA

ISBN 978-3-030-05468-7   ISBN 978-3-030-05469-4   (eBook)
https://doi.org/10.1007/978-3-030-05469-4

Cover illustration: The cover art is a depiction of an account given in Book 5 Chapter 4 of The Brothers Karamozov by Fyodor Dostoyevsky.
Cover Artwork by Justin Zimmerman.

This Palgrave Macmillan imprint is published by the registered company Springer Nature Switzerland AG
The registered company address is: Gewerbestrasse 11, 6330 Cham, Switzerland

Preface

This book attempts to provide a "logical" solution to the problem of evil in roughly the same sense that Alvin Plantinga has been thought to have provided a logical solution to the problem of evil. Plantinga and I both begin by assuming there exists a God who is all good and all powerful and then we seek to determine whether the existence of such a God is logically compatible with evil. Plantinga is widely thought to have shown that an all-good, all-powerful God is logically compatible with there being some evil in our world. What I am seeking to determine is whether or not such a God is logically compatible with the degree and amount of evil that actually exists in our world.

The search has been long and arduous. It began in 2013 after I had published my last book in political philosophy with Oxford and was considering what to do next. My work in ethics and political philosophy had developed through fifteen books and many more articles, and I was wondering how I might now continue that work. I came up with the idea of bringing ethics and political philosophy to bear on the problem of evil.

I took the idea to the John Templeton Foundation, proposing it as a project to bring the "science" of ethics to bear on philosophy of religion, specifically the problem of evil, and they were very supportive. They generously funded me to run two conferences on the topic here at Notre Dame and to research the topic myself. A conference volume was published in 2017, and now I have completed this book on the topic.

My book manuscript was originally entitled *The Problem of Evil and the Challenge of Ethics*, and what were then its first two chapters "Solving Darwin's Problems of Natural Evil" and "Eliminating the Problem of Hell," both defending solutions provisionally compatible with theism, have now been cut from the manuscript and published separately. That has made the book more unified, as indicated by its present title.

Earlier versions of the main arguments of the book were presented at the University of Notre Dame, University of Michigan, Oxford University, Rutgers University (two presentations), University of Edinburgh, Seattle University, Vanderbilt University, the University of Missouri, Fordham University, Villanova University, St. Louis University, Loyola University of Chicago, University of Oklahoma, American Philosophical Association Meetings, at two annual meetings of the Society for the Philosophy of Religion, and as a keynote address at the Contemporary Debates in Moral Philosophy Conference held in Verona, Italy. During the summer of 2018, I used the entire manuscript in a graduate seminar that I taught at Wuhan University, China.

I have clearly benefited immensely from many lengthy discussions of my work on these occasions and from even lengthier e-mail exchanges with some of those who were present after returning home. Indeed, an entire chapter (Chap. 6) was added to the manuscript after a three-month intensive back-and-forth e-mail exchange with Brian Davies of Fordham University for which I am very grateful.

I also want to specifically thank Robert Adams, Scott Aikin, Michael Almeida, Robert Audi, Michael Bergmann, Steven Boer, Kenneth Boyce, Godehard Bruentrup, Thomas Carson, Justin Christy, Nevin Climenhaga, Marilie Coetsee, Scott Coley, Edwin Curley, John Davenport, Scott Davison, Paul Draper, Evan Fales, Andrew Fiala, Thomas Flint, Bryan Frances, Jorge Garcia, Laura Garcia, Georgi Gardiner, Richard Gauser, Sherif Girgis, Elisa Grimi, Gary Gutting, John Hare, William Hasker, Frances Howard-Snyder, Benjamin Huff, Jonathan Kvanvig, Michael Scott Jones, John Lachs, Zhan Lan, Yufeng Li, Samuel Lubens, Stephen Maitzen, Edward Martin, Steven McCumber, Bradley Monton, Mark Murphy, Michael Murray, Sam Newlands, Myron Penner, Alvin Plantinga, Michael Rea, Katherin Rogers, Michael Ruse, Bruce Russell, Vincent Samar, J.L. Schellenberg, Meghan Schmitt, Josef Seifert, Kenneth

Shields, Markus Stepanians, Eleonore Stump, Meghan Sullivan, Philip Swenson, Robert Talisse, Patrick Todd, Theodore Vitali, Weiping Wang, Merold Westfall, Erik Wielenberg, Brett Wilmot, Stephen Wykstra, Niu Yau, Lisa Yount, Qing Yuan, Linda Zagzebski, Dean Zimmerman, and my philosopher's philosopher Janet Kourany for all their helpful comments and suggestions. With regard to any remaining errors and problems in my book, I definitely hope to be able to blame someone else.

Notre Dame, IN, USA   James P. Sterba

Acknowledgments

I want to thank Oxford University Press for permission to reprint from "There Is No Free-Will Defense," *Oxford Studies in Philosophy of Religion* Volume 8, September (2017) pp. 1–25, and Springer Publishing Co. to reprint from "Skeptical Theism and the Challenge of Atheism," *International Journal for Philosophy of Religion* (2018) pp. 1–19. I also want to thank the John Templeton Foundation for their generous support that started me off on the project of bringing ethics and political philosophy to bear on the problem of evil from which this book resulted.

Contents

1

Introduction

The question I seek to address in this book is whether or not an all-good God who is also presumed to be all powerful is logically possible given the degree and amount of moral evil that exists in our world.[1]

Now it is widely held by theists and atheists alike that Alvin Plantinga conclusively showed against John Mackie that it may not be within God's power to bring about a world containing moral good but no moral evil.[2] Plantinga argued that this is because to bring about a world containing moral good, God would have to permit persons to act freely, and it may well be that in every possible world where God actually permits persons to act freely, everyone would suffer from a malady such that everyone would act wrongly at least to some degree. Accepting Plantinga's defense, both theists and atheists have been willing to grant that it may be logically impossible for God to actually create a world with free agents, like ourselves, that does not also have at least some moral evil in it. Thus, it is widely agreed that a good God is logically compatible with some moral evil. Accordingly, the question I will be focusing on is whether such a God is compatible with the degree and amount of evil that actually exists in our world.

© The Author(s) 2019
J. P. Sterba, *Is a Good God Logically Possible?*,
https://doi.org/10.1007/978-3-030-05469-4_1

In recent years, discussion of the problem of evil in the world has been advanced by utilizing resources of contemporary metaphysics and episte-mology, for example, Alvin Plantinga's application of modal logic to the logical problem of evil and William Rowe, Stephen Wykstra, and Paul Draper's application of probabilistic epistemology to the evidential prob-lem of evil. The results have been impressive. What is a bit surprising, however, is that philosophers currently working on the problem of evil have yet to avail themselves of relevant resources from ethical theory that could similarly advance the discussion of the problem.[3]

For example, there is no discussion of the Doctrine of Double Effect, or whether the ends justify the means, or how to resolve hypothetical trolley cases that have become the grist for moral philosophers ever since they were introduced by Judith Thompson and Philippa Foot.[4] Even though cognitive psychologists now regularly employ hypothetical trolley cases to determine what parts of the brain are involved in the making of ethical judgments, philosophers of religion have yet to recognize the rel-evance of such cases to the problem of evil.

What is especially surprising, given that most of the defenders of the-ism in this debate are self-identified Christian philosophers, is that the central underlying element in the Doctrine of Double Effect, what has been called the Pauline Principle—Never do evil that good may come of it—has been virtually ignored by contemporary philosophers of religion despite its relevance to the problem of evil.[5]

Thus, while the principle has been a mainstay of natural law ethics at least since the time of Aquinas (notice, for example, the fundamental role it plays in the natural law ethics of John Finnis[6]), contemporary philoso-phers of religion have simply ignored it when evaluating the goods and evils that are at stake with regard to the argument from evil. Rather, they have focused on the total amount of good or evil in the world or on par-ticular horrendous evils and whether those evils can be compensated for.

It is true that the Pauline Principle has been rejected as an absolute principle. This is because there clearly are exceptions to it. Surely doing evil that good may come of it is justified when the resulting evil or harm is:

1. trivial (e.g., as in the case of stepping on someone's foot to get out of a crowded subway),

2. easily reparable (e.g., as in the case of lying to a temporarily depressed friend to keep her from committing suicide).

There is also disagreement over whether a further exception to the principle obtains when the resulting evil or harm is:

3. the only way to prevent far greater harm to innocent people (e.g., as in the case of shooting one of twenty civilian hostages to prevent, in the only way possible, the execution of all twenty).

Yet despite the recognition that there are exceptions to the principle, and despite the disagreement over the extent of those exceptions, the Pauline Principle still plays an important role in contemporary ethical theory.

Moreover, the widespread discussion of hypothetical trolley cases in contemporary ethical theory is frequently just another way of determining the range of application of the Pauline Principle. To see this, consider the following trolley case first put forward by Philippa Foot:

> A runaway trolley is headed toward five innocent people who are on the track and who will be killed unless something is done. You can redirect the trolley on to a second track, saving the five. However, on this second track is an innocent bystander who will be killed if the trolley is turned onto this track.

Is it permissible to redirect the trolley? Would that be doing evil? Clearly your redirecting the trolley would not be intentionally doing evil. What you would intentionally be doing is trying to save the five people on the track. You would not be intentionally trying to kill one to save five, although you would foresee that one person's death would definitely result from your action of saving five. So given that the Pauline Principle, properly understood, only requires that we never intentionally do evil that good may come of it, the principle does not prohibit redirecting the trolley in this case. Moreover, not only is redirecting the trolley in this case not prohibited by the Pauline Principle, it also satisfies the additional requirements for being permitted by the Doctrine of Double Effect.

Yet consider another trolley case:

> Again, there is a runaway trolley headed toward five innocent people who are on the track and who will be killed unless something is done. This time the only way for you to stop the trolley and save five is to push a big guy from a bridge onto the track.

In this case, by contrast, what you are doing, pushing the big guy onto the track, is intentionally doing evil. You are intentionally killing this large innocent person in order to save five other innocent people. Nor arguably would your action count as an exception to the Pauline Principle here, even in virtue of its contested third class of exceptions, because in this case killing one to save five would presumably be judged insufficiently beneficial to justify the killing. Thus, pushing the big guy onto the track in this case would be seen to be a violation of the Pauline Principle.

However, consider a widely discussed trolley case put forward by Bernard Williams.[7] In Williams's case, Jim, an explorer, arrives in a South American village just as Pedro, an army officer, is about have his soldiers kill a random group of twenty Indians in retaliation for protests against the local government. In honor of Jim's arrival, Pedro offers to spare nineteen of the twenty Indians, provided that Jim shoots one of them. Surely this looks like a case where the explorer should shoot one of the Indians in order to save the other nineteen. If you need to be further convinced that this type of irreparable harm to innocents can be justified for the sake of achieving greater benefit for others, then just imagine that larger and larger numbers of innocents (e.g., one hundred, one thousand, one million, whatever number you want) would be lost unless one particular (innocent) individual is killed. Surely, at some point, any defensible moral theory would justify such sacrifices for agents like ourselves.

There is then an intertwining discussion of trolley cases with the Pauline Principle which underlies the Doctrine of Double Effect that is ignored by contemporary philosophers of religion when they seek to morally evaluate the problem of evil.[8]

Today no one working on the problem of evil ever imagines backing away from the advances that Alvin Plantinga made by applying modal logic to the logical problem of evil or to the advances that William Rowe,

Stephen Wykstra, and Paul Draper made by applying probabilistic epistemology to the evidential problem of evil. All now agree that our understanding of the problem of the evil has undeniably been improved by these advances. Could it be then that by bringing to bear untapped resources of ethics on the problem of evil, there would be a similar advance in our understanding of the problem?

I think that we can expect a similar advance once we do bring to bear yet untapped resources of ethics on our understanding of the problem of evil. But I also think that this advance will be even more important than the other advances that have come from modal logic and probabilistic epistemology. This is because these other advances have really helped us more to restate the problem of evil rather than to solve it. Bringing untapped resources of ethics to bear on the problem, however, should actually help us reach a solution to the problem of evil. This is because the problem of evil is fundamentally an ethical, not a logical or epistemological, problem. Accordingly, once the relevant resources of ethical theory have been incorporated into our discussion of the problem of evil, it should be difficult to comprehend how we ever previously attempted to address the problem of evil without them.

Pursuing the goal of bringing untapped resources from ethical theory to bear on the problem of evil, two conferences were held at the University of Notre that were generously supported by the John Templeton Foundation. Marilyn McCord Adams, Laura Garcia, John Hare, Stephen Maitzen, Bruce Russell, Stephen Wykstra, and Linda Zagzebski all accepted invitations to address the thesis that there are yet untapped resources in ethical theory to better enable us to reach a solution to the problem of evil. Those who participated in the second conference had access to the papers presented at the first conference and the videoed discussion of those papers, and so they were able to use that material as a resource for their own papers, and the papers and videoed discussion from both conferences were available to all the contributors as they revised their papers for publication. I commented on all the papers. The contributors then revised their papers in light of my comments and the lively discussion of the papers we had at the conferences. These papers have now been published with an introduction and conclusion by me in the Indiana University Series in Philosophy of Religion.[9] The contributors

to this collection demonstrated in various ways the need to bring ethical theory to bear on the problem of evil.

This book attempts to more fully meet that need as follows:

Chapter 2: There Is No Free-Will Defense
In Chap. 2, I focus on a Free-Will Defense that seeks to show that God is compatible with not just some evil, but with all the evil that exists in the world, and apply an ethics of significant freedom to this version of a Free-Will Defense.

Chapter 3: An Attempt at Theodicy
In Chap. 3, I consider whether goods, other than freedom, provided in this life, or goods provided in some n-inning afterlife could morally make up for the loss of significant freedom due to God's permission of significant and especially horrendous consequences of wrongful actions.

Chapter 4: The Pauline Principle and the Just Political State
In Chap. 4, I explore whether the Pauline Principle and the analogy of an ideally just and powerful political state are compatible with God's widespread permission of significant and especially horrendous consequences of wrongful actions.

Chapter 5: Skeptical Theism to the Rescue?
In Chap. 5, I consider whether skeptical theism can successfully defend traditional theism against a logical argument from evil grounded in the fundamental requirements of our morality that are captured by exceptionless minimal components of the Pauline Principle.[10]

Chapter 6: What If God Is Not a Moral Agent?
In Chap. 6, I consider whether dropping the assumption that the God of traditional theism is a moral agent can avoid a logical argument from evil against the existence of God grounded in the fundamental requirements of our morality that are captured by exceptionless minimal components of the Pauline Principle.

Chapter 7: What About a Redemptive God?
In Chap. 7, I consider whether a justification for God's involvement with the evil in the world can be found in the long biblical history of God's seeking to bring redemption to a wayward humanity.

Chapter 8: Taking Natural Evil into Account

In Chap. 8, I examine the problem of natural evil and the challenge that it presents to the God of traditional theism.

Chapter 9: Conclusion

In Chap. 9, I review and relate the conclusions of the previous chapters, providing the most complete statement of my answer to the question the book addresses, before considering how a traditional theist should respond.

Needless to say, bringing untapped resources of ethics to bear on the problem of evil represents a new adventure in philosophy of religion that aims to achieve a resolution to the problem of evil that is nonquestion-beggingly acceptable to theists and atheists alike. Surely nothing could be more important to the future of philosophy of religion than attaining just such a resolution.

Notes

1. More precisely, the question I seek to address is whether the existence of God is logically compatible with the degree and amount of evil in the world, or, even more precisely, as I shall subsequently make clear, logically compatible with the significant and especially the horrendous evil consequences of immoral actions.
2. Responding to Plantinga's argument, Mackie himself conceded "that the problem of evil does not, after all, show that the central doctrines of theism are logically inconsistent with one another" (Mackie 1982, p. 154). William Rowe, another prominent atheist, has also endorsed Plantinga's argument. See Rowe (1979, p. 335). And numerous prominent philosophers who are theists, for example, Robert Adams and William Alston, have endorsed Plantinga's argument.
3. I do not intend to make any distinction between moral theory and ethical theory but instead treat them as synonymous.
4. According to the Doctrine of Double Effect, an action with two effects—one good and the other bad or evil—can be justified provided that the good effect is intended and the bad or evil effect is not intended but merely foreseen, and also provided that the bad or evil effect is not disproportionate to the good effect.

5. More precisely stated, as will become clear in subsequent discussion, the Pauline Principle requires us to never intentionally do moral evil that greater good may come of it.
6. See Finnis (1983, 1991, 2011a, b).
7. Judith Jarvis Thompson calls all such life-and-death hypothetical cases "trolley" cases. See Thomson (1985. pp. 1395–1415). For the case more fully set out, see Williams and Smart (1973, pp. 98–99).
8. We can also give an account of why the Pauline Principle is morally justified with its focus on prohibiting intentional harm (or evil) and its more permissive stance toward foreseen harm (or evil). It is because those who suffer harm have more reason to protest when the harm is done to them by agents who are intentionally engaged in causing harm to them than when the harm done to them is merely the foreseen consequences of actions of agents whose ends and means are good. It is also because those who cause harm have more reason to protest a restriction against foreseen harm than they do to protest a comparable restriction against intended harm. This is because a restriction against foreseen harm limits our actions when our ends and means are good, whereas a restriction against intended harm only limits our actions when our ends or means are evil or harmful, and it would seem that we have stronger grounds for acting when both our ends and means are good than when they are not. In brief, the Pauline Principle can be morally supported because we have more reason to protest when we are being used by others than when we are being affected simply by the foreseen consequences of their actions, and because we have more reason to act when both our ends and means are good than when they are not.
9. Sadly, Marilyn Adams passed away only a few days after this collection appeared in print. The last e-mail discussion I had with Marilyn on the problem of evil occurred just a few months earlier.
10. By tradition theism, I mean the form of theism which maintains that there is a creator God who is all good and all powerful, where being all knowing is subsumed under being all powerful.

Bibliography

Finnis, John. 1983. *Fundamentals of Ethics*. Washington, DC: Catholic University of America.

———. 1991. *Moral Absolutes: Tradition, Revision and Truth*. Washington, DC: Catholic University of America.

———. 2011a. *Reason in Action*. Oxford: Oxford University Press.

———. 2011b. *Human Rights and the Common Good*. Oxford: Oxford University Press.

Mackie, J.L. 1982. *The Miracle of Theism*. Oxford: Oxford University Press.

Rowe, William. 1979. The Problem of Evil and Some Varieties of Atheism. *American Philosophical Quarterly* 16: 335–341.

Thompson, Judith Jarvis. 1985. The Trolley Problem. *Yale Law Journal* 94: 1395–1415.

Williams, Bernard, and J.J.C. Smart. 1973. *Utilitarianism: For and Against*. Cambridge, UK: Cambridge University Press.

2

There Is No Free-Will Defense

In this chapter, I will employ an ethics of significant freedom to show that there is no Free-Will Defense for the degree and amount of moral evil in our world. I am not denying the Free-Will Defense that maintains it is logically possible that any world that God would create and maintain with free creatures in it is compatible with some moral evil in it as well, or, at least, I am not denying this defense given my own limited interpretation of it. Rather, I am denying that God's creating and maintaining our world with the degree and amount of moral evil that exists, or has existed, in it could be defended in terms of the freedom that it provides, or has provided, to its members. However, I am not denying that God's creating and maintaining our world with all its evil could be justified on other grounds. Accordingly, it may be argued that the securing of some other moral good, or goods, in this life or in an afterlife is the justification for the degree and amount of moral evil in our world. I am not contesting that possibility. My primary thesis here is simply that the freedom that exists, or has existed, in our world could not constitute a justification for the moral evil that exists, or has existed, in it. However, my secondary thesis is that Plantinga has not succeeded in showing that God is logically compatible even with some evil in the world, when that evil is taken to

© The Author(s) 2019
J. P. Sterba, *Is a Good God Logically Possible?*,
https://doi.org/10.1007/978-3-030-05469-4_2

be, as it may well be, any of the significant and especially the horrendous consequences of our immoral actions.

It should be noted that Plantinga understands important or significant freedom in a broader way than I am here. For Plantinga, to be significantly free is to be free with respect to an action that is morally significant, which is an action it would be wrong for an agent to perform but right to refrain from performing or vice versa.[1] For me, significant freedoms are those freedoms a just political state would want to protect since that would fairly secure each person's fundamental interests. Both of us, however, understand significant freedoms to include inner freedoms, such as the freedom to imagine, intend and even to take the initial wrongful steps toward bringing about significant and even horrendous consequences of immoral action on would-be victims.

God, of course, could secure for us significant freedom in my sense and/or significant freedom in Plantinga's sense, but there is more justification for God, like the just political state, to focus on securing significant freedom in my sense. Significant freedoms for me are like the freedom from assault, whereas Plantinga's significant freedoms include those freedoms and also include freedoms like the freedom of not having someone cut in front of us in the line for the movies. Clearly, it is God's failure to secure significant freedoms in my sense and not God's failure to secure the additional freedoms also captured by Plantinga's more expansive notion of significant freedom that gives rise to the problem of evil. This is because God's failure to secure the additional freedoms included under Plantinga's sense of significant freedom, just like the just political state's failure to secure such freedoms, is entirely morally appropriate, even morally required. Hence, the need to focus on freedoms that are significant freedoms in my sense and not on those additional freedoms that are also included under Plantinga's more expansive notion of significant freedom when we are dealing with the problem of evil in the world.

I

My argument begins by noting that political states, particularly those aiming at securing a high level of justice for their members, are structured to secure a range of important freedoms for all their members, even when doing so requires interfering with the freedoms of some of their members. For example, consider the laws against assault. Such laws are designed to help protect people against assault, where assault is understood characteristically as intentionally acting to cause serious physical injury to another person. These laws are thus designed to help secure freedom from assault by attempting to prevent assaults whenever possible, and when assaults do occur, they assist with additional provisions for apprehending perpetrators and restricting their freedom in appropriate ways. Such laws are clearly not structured so as never to interfere with the freedom of any of their members.

Thus, suppose that Nat, a law enforcement officer, is responding to an emergency call in a political state whose laws purport to secure a high level of justice, and she comes upon Matt who is about to assault Pat, his domestic partner. Here there is no question that Nat would take steps to stop Matt from carrying out his assault on Pat. She would not be concerned to allow Matt the freedom to carry out the harmful consequences of his act. Rather, she would be concerned to secure Pat's freedom from Matt's assault. The freedom of Matt to carry out his assault would have virtually no weight at all against Pat's freedom not to be assaulted by Matt.

Moreover, whenever such assaults occur, they result in a morally unacceptable distribution of freedom. What happens is that the freedom of the assaulters, a freedom no one should have, is exercised at the expense of the freedom of their victims not to be assaulted, an important freedom that everyone should have.

Of course, even in just states, people can still fantasize about assaulting others. Think about Jackie Gleason's character, Ralph Kramden in *The Honeymooners*, fantasizing about what he would do to his wife, Alice, played by Audrey Meadows.[2] People can even intend to carry out assaults, and take very general, multiple-use preparatory steps to do so. Yet it is only when they take clear steps toward committing an assault that normally they are interfered with in societies that purport to be just.

Of course, not infrequently, even political states intent upon securing justice for their members are unsuccessful at constraining the freedom of would-be assaulters and protecting the freedom of their would-be victims. And there are many political states that are far less concerned about securing justice for their members where law enforcement officers just allow assaults to be committed, or even participate in carrying them out themselves. Still, the practice of constraining the freedom of would-be assaulters in favor of the freedom of their would-be victims is character-istic of societies that are strongly concerned to be just.

II

Now in the law, assaults are acts that cause serious injury and thus impose significant evils on their victims. But are these evils horrendous evils? Marilyn Adams defines horrendous evils as evils "the participation in which (that is, the doing or suffering of which) constitutes prima facie reason to doubt whether the participant's life could (given their inclusion in it) be a great good to him/her on the whole" (Adams 1999, p. 26). While some assaults impose horrendous evils, as Adams defines them, some do not. Nor are horrendous evils, so defined, just a subclass of assaults. One reason for this is that some horrendous evils are the result of natural disasters, and so are not the result of assaults at all. Moreover, given that my focus is on the Free-Will Defense of moral evil, I am not concerned with outcomes, even horrendously evil ones, which are simply the result of natural forces. Rather, I am concerned with the significant moral evil that results from human freedom or the lack thereof.[3]

It might be objected here that I cannot separate off natural evils in the way I propose because God, unlike humans, could be held to be morally responsible for natural evils.[4] But while this objection has some merit, I propose to set it aside here, and simply focus on the question of whether a Free-Will Defense can exonerate God from responsibility for the moral evil in the world.[5] So my attention is directed only at those significant moral evils that have their origin in human freedom and the lack thereof.

III

This means that the evils I am concerned with represent a broader class of evils than those that simply result from assaults. In assaults, a free-dom no one should have is obtained by sacrificing the freedom of their victims to be without such assaults, which is an important freedom that everyone should have. This results in a morally unacceptable distribution of freedom in society. But obviously morally unacceptable distributions of freedom can come about by means other than assaults. So we need to consider not just significant moral evils that result from assaults but the broader class of significant moral evils that have their origin in human freedom and the lack thereof.

To better appreciate this broader range of evils, consider conflicts between the rich and the poor. In these conflict situations, the rich, of course, have more than enough resources to satisfy their basic needs. In contrast, imagine that the poor lack the resources to meet their basic needs to secure a decent life for themselves even though they have tried all the means available to them that libertarians, who value freedom above all, regard as legitimate for acquiring such resources.[6]

Now the lack of resources to meet their basic needs clearly constitutes a significant evil for the poor. However, whether it is a moral evil or not depends on whether the poor are morally entitled to such resources.[7] So it is relevant that under circumstances like these, libertarians maintain that the rich should have the freedom to use their resources to satisfy their luxury needs if they so wish. Libertarians recognize that this freedom might well be enjoyed with the consequence that the satisfaction of the basic needs of the poor will not be met; they just think that freedom always has priority over other political ideals, and since they assume that the freedom of the poor is not at stake in such conflict situations, it is easy for them to conclude that the rich should not be required to sacrifice their freedom so that the basic needs of the poor may be met. According to libertarians, therefore, the poor's lack of resources is not a moral evil imposed on them by the rich.

Of course, libertarians allow that it would be nice of the rich to share their surplus resources with the poor. Nevertheless, according to libertarians, such acts of charity are not required because the freedom of the poor is not thought to be at stake in such conflict situations. So, at least initially, libertarians do not see the poor as suffering from a moral evil at the hands of the rich because they do not see the freedom of the poor at stake in their conflict with the rich. As libertarians see it, the conflict is simply one between the freedom of the rich and the needs of the poor.

It turns out that libertarians are wrong about the conflict between the rich and the poor. They are right to see it as a conflict between the freedom of the rich and the needs of the poor. What they fail to see is that it is also a conflict between the freedom of the rich and the freedom of the poor. The freedom of the poor is truly at stake in such conflict situations with the rich. What is at stake is the freedom of the poor not to be interfered with in taking from the surplus possessions of the rich what is necessary to satisfy their basic needs.

Needless to say, libertarians want to deny that the poor have this freedom. But how can they justify such a denial? As this freedom of the poor has been specified, it is not a positive freedom to receive something but a negative freedom of noninterference. Clearly, what libertarians must do is recognize the existence of such a freedom and then claim that it unjustifiably conflicts with other freedoms of the rich. But when libertarians see that this is the case, they are often genuinely surprised for they had not previously seen the conflict between the rich and the poor as a conflict of freedoms.[8]

Now when the conflict between the rich and the poor is viewed as a conflict of freedoms, we can either say that the rich should have the freedom not to be interfered with in using their surplus resources for luxury purposes, or we can say that the poor should have the freedom not to be interfered with in taking from the rich what they require to meet their basic needs. If we choose one freedom, we must reject the other. What needs to be determined, therefore, is which freedom is morally enforceable: the freedom of the rich or the freedom of the poor.

Elsewhere, I have argued that the freedom of the poor, which is the freedom not to be interfered with in taking from the surplus resources of the rich what is required to meet one's basic needs, is morally enforceable over the freedom of the rich, which is the freedom not to be interfered with in using one's surplus resources for luxury purposes.[9] This means that within the bundle of freedoms allotted to each person by the basic principle of libertarianism, there must be the freedom not to be interfered with (when one is poor) in taking from the surplus possessions of the rich what is necessary to satisfy one's basic needs. I argue that this must be part of the bundle that constitutes the greatest amount of freedom for each person because this freedom is morally superior to the freedom with which it directly conflicts, that is, the freedom not to be interfered with (when one is rich) in using one's surplus possessions to satisfy one's luxury needs.

So my argument is that a libertarian ideal of freedom by favoring the freedom of the poor over the freedom of the rich can be seen to support a right to welfare. Assuming further that we can meaningfully speak of distant peoples and future generations as having rights against us and we corresponding obligations to them, there is no reason not to extend my argument for a right to welfare to distant peoples and future generations. This is because for libertarians, fundamental rights are universal rights, that is, rights possessed by all people, not just those who live in certain places or at certain times.

Of course, to claim that rights are universal does not mean that they are universally recognized. Rather, to claim that rights are universal, despite their spotty recognition, implies only that they ought to be recognized because people at all times and places have or could have had good reasons to recognize these rights, not that they actually did or do so.

Nor need universal rights be unconditional. This is particularly true in the case of the right to welfare, which is conditional upon people doing all that they reasonably can be expected to do to provide for themselves. In addition, this right is conditional upon there being sufficient resources available so that everyone's welfare needs can be met. So where people do not do all that they can reasonably be expected to do to provide for themselves or where there are not sufficient resources available, people do not normally have a right to welfare.

Given the universal and conditional character of this libertarian right to welfare, I argue that this right should be extended to distant peoples, and I agree with Peter Singer that this can be done at minimal costs to the rich. But, unlike Singer, I don't stop with distant peoples. I further argue that this right should be extended to future generations. The upshot is that until we have a technological fix, recognizing a universal right to welfare applicable to both existing and future people requires us to use up no more resources than are necessary for meeting our own basic needs, thus securing for ourselves a decent life but no more. For us to use up more resources than this, without a technological fix, we would be guilty of depriving at least some future generations of the resources they would require to meet their own basic needs, thereby violating their libertarian-based right to welfare. Obviously, this would impose a significant sacrifice on existing generations, particularly those in the developed world, clearly a far greater sacrifice than Singer maintains is required for meeting the basic needs of existing generations. Nevertheless, these demands do follow from a libertarian-based right to welfare. In effect, then, recognizing a right to welfare, applicable to all existing and future people, leads to an equal utilization of resources over place and time.

Now my argument is that the libertarian ideal of freedom leads to a right to welfare which, of course, welfare liberals endorse, and that this right to welfare extended to distant peoples and future generations leads to the equality that socialists endorse. Assuming that my argument is correct, it shows how far we are from a morally defensible distribution of significant freedom in most societies across the world, and that this has been true throughout most of human history.[10]

Yet even if one did not accept my argument, it would still be hard to reject its conclusion that we have not yet achieved a morally acceptable distribution of significant freedom in most societies around the world and that this has been true throughout most of human history. As we noted earlier, even in political states that aim at securing a high level of justice for their members, their laws against assault still operate imperfectly, and thus result in a distribution of freedom that is unjust to some degree. The problem is more severe when we consider the effect that significant evils other than assaults have on the distribution of freedom in society. Here I would maintain, particularly in the economic arena, that the rate of failure even in political states that aim to be just is much more pronounced, because, unlike cases of assault, the maldistribution of significant freedom is less easy to see. Of course, problems are much more severe in political states that are far less, or not at all, concerned about justice for their members. Accordingly, we humans have almost always lived in societies that are marred, or even characterized, by unjust distributions of freedom. We either have brought about the injustice ourselves, simply benefited from it, or even when not benefiting from it have not done what we can to correct it. Alternatively, we ourselves may be the victims who are suffering under injustice. In any case, that there is an unjust distribution of freedom in virtually all societies around the world and that this has been true for most of human history seem difficult to challenge.

The clear upshot is that we humans are at least partially responsible for the unjust distribution of freedom that has characterized human history. The world would be far more just if many of us acted differently, if we did more to bring about a just society. There is no escaping the blame that many of us bear. We could do better, but we don't, and people in the past could have done better as well.

IV

Suppose, however, there were among us persons with superhuman powers for making our societies more just than they are. Suppose comic book and cinematic persons like Superman, Wonder Woman, Spider-Man, and Xena really did exist. What would we expect of them? Would we not expect them to do what they can to make our societies more just than they are, and thereby bring about a better distribution of significant freedom?

It is true that these fictional superheroes are often pitted against super-villains who rival them in power. However, from time to time, these superheroes are shown coming up against ordinary villains, and it just takes a minimal exercise of their superhuman powers for them to prevent significant evils from occurring, thereby securing significant freedoms for those who would otherwise suffer those evils. And when that happens, no one really protests, except possibly the villains themselves. In fact, inaction by the superheroes in such contexts is broadly condemned by virtually everyone, again, save the villains themselves.

Spider-Man/Peter Parker, for example, is exercised by the motto: with great power, there must also come great responsibility. It is in fact pressed upon him by his Uncle Ben who raised him, just before his uncle dies in a tragic set of circumstances that result, in part, from Spider-Man's initial failure to live by that motto. After the death of his uncle, Spider-Man does strive to live by the motto, and his main problem becomes how to do so while still maintaining some kind of a personal life. Similar commitments are also made by other superheroes, although they too have comparable difficulties figuring out how to live by those commitments while maintaining a personal life.

Nevertheless, among superheroes, the idea that they should limit the freedom of would-be villains to protect would-be victims is just taken for granted. Of course, superheroes are more frequently shown protecting people from serious assault. They are less frequently portrayed as protecting people from the significant evils of an unjust economic system, thereby securing people's freedom in that area of their lives. This may be because showing just transfers of income from the rich to the poor do not tend to make great theater. One place where this has been effectively dramatized, however, is in the semi-fictional account of the adventures of Robin Hood, where a dispossessed nobleman, Robin of Loxley, fights against the attempt by the Sheriff of Nottingham to deprive, especially poor people, of their rightful property. So inspiring is this moral tale that the hero's name has come to be applied to virtually anyone who uses extra-legal, but justified, means to transfer economic resources from the rich to the poor. Thus, at least in the world of comic book and cinematic superheroes, much is done to bring about a more just distribution of significant freedoms in society, and we, who also imaginatively live in that world, generally think this is the way it should be.[11]

V

Why then, in the actual world, couldn't God, like the superheroes in our fictional world, be more involved in preventing evils that result in the loss of significant freedom for their victims?

Consider the case of Matthew Shepard who was befriended by two men in a bar in Laramie, Wyoming, in 1998. The two men, who were reportedly anti-gay, offered to give Shepard a lift and then drove him to a remote location where they robbed, severely beat, and tortured him, and then left him to die hanging on a fence, where he lapsed into unconsciousness and was discovered the next day by a passing cyclist who thought he was a scarecrow. Shepard died two days later in a Laramie hospital never having regained consciousness.[12]

Surely God could have intervened in this case, maybe just by causing the car Shepard was in to have a flat tire as it was being driven out of the bar's parking lot. Then Shepard could have gotten a ride with someone else or walked to his lodging near the University of Wyoming campus where he was a first year student. If God had done this, Shepard's two assailants would still have been able to freely imagine, intend, and even take initial steps toward carrying out their presumably anti-gay motivated robbery, torture, and murder of Shepard. They would just have been prevented from carrying out the final step of their action with its horrible consequences for their victim. Their freedom not to be interfered with in taking action to bring about the anti-gay motived robbery, torture, and murder of Matthew Shepard would surely have been restricted by God's causing them to have a flat tire. But clearly that was not an important freedom for them to have. Even the legal authorities in Laramie had taken steps to prevent their residents from exercising such freedoms. Their enforcement system was just not that effective. The authorities surely did not think that would-be assailants should have the freedom to assault their intended victims.

Consider as well the very significant freedom Matthew Shepard would have enjoyed if the freedom of his would-be assailants had been restricted in this regard. He would have enjoyed the freedom not to be assaulted, tortured, and murdered which would have presumably led to his enjoying other freedoms such as the freedom to complete his education and the freedom to find meaningful work.[13] Surely, these and other freedoms that Shepard would have enjoyed if his assault had been prevented are a lot more important than the freedom his assailants exercised. This is clearly why virtually no one would protest the action of a superhero who would prevent the harmful consequences of the actions of Shepard's would-be assailants in order to secure such important freedoms for Shepard. There seems to be no question about what a more morally justified distribution of freedom would look like in this case.

VI

Yet what if God, a superhero, or someone else had intervened and prevented Shepard's murder so that he was able to continue on with his life. Suppose that Shepard later chose to be a pro-gay vigilante who sought out people with anti-gay sentiments and did to them what his unsuccessful assailants had intended to do to him. Would this then show that failing to prevent Shepard's assault would have been justified because it would have resulted in preventing the far more horrendous evils that Shepard would have gone on to commit himself?

Surely this does raise a problem with regard to the justification for preventing the assault on Shepard. However, the appropriate solution would not be for God or someone with superhuman powers to permit the assault against Shepard, but rather for the intervener to go on to prevent any further significant assaults by Shepard that he would attempt in the future. In each such case, the intervention would restrict a not very important freedom of the would-be assailant in order to secure significant freedoms for those who would otherwise be victims. Surely, that would be the best way to bring about a morally defensible distribution of freedom in this regard.

Consider a different scenario. Consider the possibility that allowing the loss of significant freedoms in the present could lead to a gain in significant freedoms in the future. So in the case of Matthew Shepard, imagine that the loss of significant freedom for Shepard could lead to the gain of significant freedom in the future that logically could not be attained in any other way. Actually, as things turned out, this was, in fact, the case. Shepherd's death did result in the freedom for Shepard's mother to respond to his death by building support for a federal law that better protected gays and lesbians from discrimination as well as the freedom for Shepard's assailants to respond to his death by repenting their actions and reforming themselves. Although it does not appear that Shepard's assailants took advantage of these freedoms, they were still available to them. However, these freedoms, even taken together, are in no way as significant as the freedoms that Shepard lost, and so they alone could not justify that loss. Moreover, something like these same freedoms would still have been available to Shepard's mother and to his assailants even if Shepard had not suffered his horrible loss. Thus, Shepard's mother would still have had the freedom, maybe this time in cooperation with her son, to take on the task of building support for a federal law that better protected gays and lesbians from discrimination. Likewise, Shepard's assailants would still have had the freedom to repent their discriminatory ways and reform themselves, even if they had not murdered Shepard. Hence, the only way that allowing Shepard's loss of significant freedom could ever possibly be justified in terms of freedom is if that loss had been logically necessary to secure a greater gain in comparable freedoms.

Thus, suppose you are in circumstances where if you intervened to stop a deadly assault on someone, you end up exposing a large group of people to the same kind of deadly assault. Surely, in such circumstances, given your lack of power to effect a better resolution, you would be justified in allowing the deadly assault on the one person. But even in this case the justification is provided by causal necessity not by the logical necessity that would be required to justify God's permission in the Matthew Shepard case. Moreover, the particular freedoms of Shepard's mother and his assailants that are logically connected to his murder are clearly not as important as the freedoms that Shepard would lose in order for them to possess those freedoms, as would be true of any freedoms that were logically connected to the freedoms that Shepard would lose by being murdered. Indeed, as we noted, there are comparable freedoms that Shepard's mother and his assailants would have had without the loss of his life. Even if there was a causal chain extending from Shepard's murder through the action of his mother in building support for a federal law that better protected gays and lesbians to an actual reduction of deadly assaults on gays and lesbians, there is nothing logically necessary in such a train of events. Surely, an omni-God, or even humans operating under circumstances where Shepard's murder had been prevented, could have achieved those same good results. So clearly for God, and even for us, there was no way that failing to prevent Matthew Shepard's murder could have been justified in terms of a gain in significant freedom when compared to the loss of significant freedom that resulted from his murder.[14]

So clearly with respect to the broad range of actual cases in the world, God has not chosen to secure the freedoms of those who are morally entitled to those freedoms by restricting others from exercising freedoms that they are not morally entitled to exercise. As a consequence, significant moral evil has resulted that could otherwise have been prevented. So if God is justified in permitting such moral evils, it has to be on grounds other than freedom because an assessment of the freedoms that are at stake would require God to act preventively to secure a morally defensible distribution of freedom, which, of course, God has not done. So if God is to be justified with respect to cases like Matthew Shepard's, it must be because there is a justification for God's inaction in terms other than freedom. It would have to be a justification for permitting moral evil on the grounds that it secures some other good or goods in this life, or other goods in an afterlife. Now I am not contesting the possibility of that sort of a justification for the moral evil in our world here.[15] What I am claiming here is simply that the freedom that exists, or has existed, or even will exist, in our world could not constitute the justification for the moral evil that exists, or has existed, in it.[16] My claim is simply that there is no Free-Will Defense of the moral evil that exists in this world now or in the past.

It might be objected that if the freedom of would-be assailant's freedom is unconstrained, they may undergo a moral transformation and deeply regret and seek forgivingness for their wrongdoing. Now while the freedom to commit a serious wrong and then later repent having done so is a freedom of some significance, it does not have priority over the freedom not to be seriously wronged in the first place. No just political state is going to deny people the first freedom so that others can benefit from the second.[17]

VII

Yet how does my argument against the Free-Will Defense relate to Plantinga's attempt to advance that defense beyond his solution to the so-called logical problem of evil?[18] Plantinga's solution to the so-called logical problem of evil depends on the claim that it may not be within God's power to bring about a world containing moral good but no moral evil. Plantinga argued that this is because to bring about a world containing moral good, God would have to permit persons he creates to act freely, and it may well be that in every world where God actually permits persons he creates to act freely, every one of them would suffer from a malady that Plantinga labeled Transworld Depravity (TD), and so every one of them would act wrongly at least to some degree. However, Richard Otte has shown that given Plantinga's original definition of TD, it is necessarily false that all the persons God creates would suffer from TD (Otte 2009). Otte went on to helpfully offer a different definition of TD that is free of this logical difficulty (Ibid.). Yet other philosophers have questioned whether TD, however formulated, is any more plausible than Transworld Sanctity (TS), an opposing view that holds that necessarily at least one person in any world God actualized would never act wrongly.[19] Faced with such dissension, Plantinga has entertained another suggestion from Otte that all he really needs to counter the argument from evil posed by John Mackie is simply to espouse the One Wrong Thesis (OW), which just claims that if God tried to actualize a morally perfect world, at least one person he creates would act wrongly (Otte 2009, p. 173ff). Thus, OW makes no assumption, as TD does, about how all persons God creates would act.

No doubt, OW is far more plausible than TD, and thus more useful for a solution to the so-called logical problem of evil. Nevertheless, I think there is a better way to approach the problem of evil posed by Mackie. The general approach favored by Plantinga and others has seemed to come up with possible constraints on God's power that would serve to account for evil in the world. Yet what about seeing evil in the world as required by God's goodness rather than simply being required by constraints on God's power?[20] Surely, we have no difficulty seeing at least some of the moral evil in the world in this light. Think, for example, of your not being fully honest with a temporarily depressed friend to keep him from doing something he would deeply regret later.[21] Arguably, a good God would have no difficulty permitting (hence, not interfering with) such minor moral wrongs, given a greater good that might result or a greater evil that would thereby be prevented. That admission might seem to be all that is needed to solve the problem of evil posed by Mackie. It is a solution based on an appeal to God's goodness rather than simply to any constraint on God's power.[22] So the idea is to appeal to God's goodness to explain why God's power has not been exercised in a certain regard rather than appeal to (a limitation of) God's power to explain why God has not done some particular good.

Notice that underlying this alternative approach to the problem of evil posed by Mackie is a commitment to the following moral principle:

Noninterference (NI)

Every moral agent has reason not to interfere with the free actions of wrongdoers when permitting the slightly harmful consequences of those actions would lead to securing some significant moral good, in some cases, maybe just that of the freedom of the wrongdoers themselves, or to preventing some significant moral evil.[23]

NI holds of ourselves, but it also holds of God, and, on that account, it permits a solution to the problem of evil posed by Mackie when the evil that we seeking to reconcile with God's existence is the "slightly harmful consequences of wrongdoing."

Yet what about when the evil is not the slightly harmful consequences of wrongdoing but rather the significant and especially the horrendous consequences of such wrongdoing, as it may well be? In that case, NI will not serve to justify noninterference with the free actions of wrongdoers. Thus, in order for such noninterference to be justified, or possibly justified, in such cases, more needs to be established, or possibly established, about a greater evil that would be prevented or a greater good that would be achieved by permitting the evil consequences in such cases. In such cases, we need a much stronger justification, or possible justification, in terms of the prevention of a greater evil or the provision of a greater good to hold in order for the permission of evil to be justified, or possibly justified. Yet Plantinga by appealing simply to the freedom of the wrongdoer alone as a justification, or possible justification, has not achieved this. Something else would be needed that Plantinga does not provide. Consequently, Plantinga has not succeeded in showing with his Free-Will Defense that the existence of God is logically compatible with even some moral evil in the world, particularly when the evil in question is, as it may well be, the significant and especially the horrendous consequences of immoral actions. Plantinga needs to provide a greater good justification, or possible justification, particularly for God's permitting significant and especially horrendous evil consequences of wrongdoing other than by simply appealing to the freedom of the wrongdoers, given that these are consequences that God, and you or I on occasion, could easily prevent. And Plantinga has not done this.

Even if we were to focus on the freedoms that are at issue here, we see that more freedoms than Plantinga takes into account are relevant to the problem of evil. Thus, when Plantinga attempts to use his Free-Will Defense to show that the existence of God is logically compatible not just with some moral evil but with all the evil in our world, he imagines God creating us and placing us in a situation where we are free, and where the amount of moral evil that exists in the world is simply the result of how we exercise that freedom. Plantinga assumed that God cannot act otherwise without reducing the freedom in the world and thereby also reducing the moral good that comes from exercising that freedom. Yet Plantinga fails to take into account that there are two ways that God can promote freedom in the world. He recognizes that God can promote freedom by not interfering with our free actions. However, he fails to recognize that God can also promote freedom, in fact, promote far greater significant freedom, by actually interfering with the freedom of some of our free actions at certain times. God's relevant activity for Plantinga appears to be limited to simply creating us and making us free. For Plantinga, what happens after that, particularly the evil consequences that result from our actions, is our responsibility, not God's. Yet it is far more plausible to see an all-good, all-powerful God as also interacting with us continually over time, always having the option of either interfering or not interfering with our actions, and especially with the consequences of our actions.[24]

Of course, the same holds true for ourselves. We frequently have the option of interfering or not interfering with the freedom of others, and we have to decide what we should do. Because Plantinga failed to see that God, in particular, can promote more significant freedom over time by sometimes interfering with our free actions, he failed to see that the problem of the compatibility of God and the degree and amount of moral evil that actually exists in the world is not settled by just noting God's act of creation and placing us in an initial situation where we are free. We have to further take into account the extent to which God has promoted freedom by restricting the far less significant freedom of some of us in order to secure the far more significant freedom of others.

Nor would it do to claim that the freedom relied upon by the Free-Will Defense is contra-causal freedom, not the freedom as noninterference cherished by political libertarians. This is because contra-causal freedom presupposes freedom as noninterference: you cannot be contra-causally free to do X if you are interfered with such that you are kept from doing X. To have contra-causal freedom, you must have freedom as noninterference as well. Moreover, if you lack the contra-causal freedom to do X, according to the defenders of this analysis of freedom, this is frequently because you also lack the freedom of noninterference with respect to doing X. Nevertheless, for defenders of this analysis of freedom, there can be other explanations for the lack of contra-causal freedom, such as inner compulsions or crippling fears. Still, the connection between contra-causal freedom and freedom as noninterference is understood to be quite close, and supporters of the Free-Will Defense must acknowledge that this is the case.[25] The loss of the one sort of freedom is tantamount to a loss of the other; a gain in the one is tantamount to a gain in the other.

Nor would it do to claim that the freedom that is at issue here is an inner freedom of the will that could not be effected at all by external intervention. This is because if that were the only freedom that was at issue here, God could have prevented all the evil in the world without interfering with this freedom at all. Thus, freedom in this sense provides no grounds at all for why God does not intervene.[26]

Nor does my critique of the Free-Will Defense depend on there being counterfactuals of freedom to which God would have access. In fact, the whole Molinist debate in philosophy of religion turns out to be irrelevant to my critique. For my critique to work, God doesn't need to be able to determine our internal free acts, something that if indeterminism is true, even God may not be able to do, according to Molinism. Rather, for my critique to work, God simply needs to be able to prevent the external consequences of our significant and especially horrendous immoral acts, something that superheroes or we ourselves, when well placed, should be able to do.

Even on a contra-causal account of free action, there is a point where the significantly evil consequences of free acts have a purely causal history (their contra-causal origins coming before this purely causal history begins). At that point, an omniscient and all-powerful God would surely be aware of these causal processes as they get going to divert them or put a stop to them. In so doing, God would be interfering with the less significant freedom of would-be wrongdoers for the sake of securing the more significant freedom of their would-be victims.

VIII

Now we have seen that political states, especially those that aim to achieve a certain degree of justice, are committed to restricting the far less significant freedoms of would-be aggressors in order to secure the far more significant freedoms of their would-be victims. We have also seen that political states can restrict freedoms in other areas, particularly the economic sphere, with the same justification for promoting more significant freedoms. And something similar holds true for us as individuals. We too have options to promote greater and more significant freedoms by restricting some people's lesser freedoms.

In our imaginations, we have also taken on the task of promoting significant freedoms by conceiving of superheroes restricting the freedoms of ordinary villains to prevent them from restricting the more significant freedoms of their would-be victims. Given that there is much that political states and individuals still have not done to promote significant freedom in the world, superheroes manage to play an important role in our imaginations bringing about a more just distribution of significant freedom than exists in the world as we find it. For many of us, the role that superheroes play in our imaginations closely parallels the role we ourselves think we should play in the actual world if we only had the superhuman powers to do so.

Accordingly, the actual world we live in is such that there is much more that God could have done to promote significant freedom in it. The problem is not with God's creating us and giving us free will. Rather, the real problem comes later in time when God fails to restrict the lesser freedoms of wrongdoers to secure the more significant freedoms of their victims. Hence, the world we live in cannot be justified by the distribution and amount of significant freedom that is in it. There are too many ways that political states and human individuals could have increased the amount of significant freedom by restricting lesser freedoms of would-be wrongdoers. Likewise, there is much that God could have done to promote freedom by restricting freedom that simply has not been done.

So we cannot say that God's justification for permitting the moral evil in the world is the freedom that is in it because God could have reduced the moral evil in the world by increasing the significant freedom in the world, and that has not been done. Hence, there is no Free-Will Defense of the degree and amount of moral evil in the world. Nor has Plantinga even provided a Free-Will Defense for some evil in the world when that evil is taken to be any of the significant and especially the horrendous consequences of our immoral actions. Accordingly, if the moral evil in the world is justified, it cannot be because of the freedom in the world because God could have decreased the moral evil in the world by justifiably restricting the freedoms of some to promote significant freedoms for others. Accordingly, if there is a justification for the moral evil in the world that renders it compatible with the existence of God, it has to be in terms of something other than the distribution and amount of freedom in our world. The justification would have to be provided in terms of securing of some other good, or goods. Once then it is settled that there is no Free-Will Defense for the moral evil in this world, we need to take up the question of whether the moral principles or requirements that govern the production and distribution of other goods can serve to justify God's permission of the degree and amount of moral evil in the world as we know it. If we are successful in finding such a justification, we will have a defense of the degree and amount of moral evil in the world. But it will not be a Free-Will Defense.

Still, a critic might respond that while I have shown that the degree and amount of moral evil that exists in the world cannot be justified by the distribution and amount of freedom in it, I have not, by my own admission, shown that the evil could not be justified by the amount and distribution of moral goods other than freedom in this world or in an afterlife. This is true. But if this is all that the Free-Will Defense wanted to hold then the view is surely mischaracterized as a "Free-Will Defense," and should really be called a Greater Moral Good Defense, since it concedes that our world has considerably less significant freedom in it than God could have otherwise effected. Moreover, this Greater Moral Good Defense itself requires a defense. There is a need to show that moral principles or requirements binding on ourselves and on God would permit the tradeoff of our significant freedoms in our world in order to secure greater moral goods. Accordingly, even allowing that I have shown that there that really is no Free-Will Defense, it remains to be seen whether there is a Greater Moral Good Defense for the lack of significant freedom and the consequent greater moral evil that exists in our world.[27]

Notes

1. See Plantinga (1974, p. 30).
2. Part of the humor in *The Honeymooners* was that both characters "knew," Alice from her wiser perspective, that Ralph would never do, or even intend to do, what he was fantasizing about doing.
3. I understand "significant moral evils that have their origin in the lack of freedom" to themselves have resulted, in turn, from morally wrong actions because otherwise they would not be lacks of freedom but lacks of something else.
4. This is too strong. Humans too can be responsible for natural evils, as presently is the case through the human impact on climate change.
5. The problem of natural evil will be discussed in Chap. 8.
6. By "libertarians" here I mean "political libertarians" who, as I say in the text, value freedom above all. Accordingly, they also endorse the ideal that each person should have the greatest amount of freedom morally commensurate with the greatest amount of freedom for everyone else. The political libertarian is thus different from the metaphysical libertarian who endorses contra-causal freedom. However, in section VII, I show how the two are closely related. There are also other kinds of "political libertarians" who do not value freedom about all, and there are still other forms of libertarianism, such as civil libertarianism and neolibertarianism to which I am not referring.
7. I think this is right. Assume that others should help you out in some regard, but only in a supererogatory sense. This would mean that you are not entitled to that help and others are not obligated to provide it. It does not seem then that the failure of others to provide that help would be a moral evil. It would be morally good for them to help you out, but their not doing so is not morally bad, and hence, it is not a moral evil.
8. See Machan (2006, Chapter 20), Mack (1991, pp. 64–72), Narveson (2001, p. 35).
9. Most recently, in Sterba (2014).
10. Although prehistoric humans did not aggress against their natural environments as much as we do today, they did unnecessarily drive many species into extinction and thereby threaten the basic needs of future generations, and they also failed to secure a morally acceptable distribution of freedom in their existing in-group and between-group relations.
11. For more on the role superheroes have in our moral imagination, see Oropeza (2008) and Morris and Morris, editors (2005).

12. For more on the Matthew Shepard story, see Shepard (2009). There is now conflicting evidence surrounding exactly why Matthew Shepard was killed. At the trial, there was testimony that the two men "just wanted to beat [Shepard] up bad enough to teach him a lesson not to come on to straight people," but now there is other evidence brought to light by Stephen Jimenez (2013) that drugs may have figured importantly in the killing. However, the exact motives of Shepard's killers are not relevant to determining the net loss of significant freedoms resulting from his death, which is what I am concerned about here.

13. These last two freedoms should be more fully expressed as the freedom not to be interfered with in completing an education and the freedom not to be interfered with in finding meaningful work.

14. Moreover, as we shall see later, even if such gains in comparable freedom were possible, they would still be morally objectionable because their would-be beneficiaries would morally prefer not to have them.

15. I will be examining that possibility in subsequent chapters.

16. Strong as the argument is here that there is no defense in terms of freedom for God's permission of significant and especially horrendous consequences of wrongful acts; an even stronger argument will be given for this conclusion in subsequent chapters which relies on a jointly exhaustive classification of the possible goods with which we can be provided.

17. It should be clear from my discussion, and especially from my introduction of the analogy of a ideally just and powerful state, that I am assuming that my preferred solution for the Shepard case needs to be generalized and applied to all relevantly similar cases. Whether this creates a problem for my view will be addressed in subsequent chapters.

18. I refer here to "the so-called logical problem of evil" because, as I explain below, the proposed solution I favor depends on a moral requirement that applies to both God and ourselves and to the logical relations of that principle to the circumstances in which we find ourselves. Now it may turn out that a defensible solution to the problem of evil that takes into account the degree and amount of evil in the world also depends on the logical relations between moral requirements and the circumstances in which we find ourselves. If so, we would not have any good reason to call one problem of evil a logical problem, but not the other.

19. See Howard-Snyder (2013) and Howard-Snyder and O'Leary-Hawthorne (1998). See also Pruss (2012) and Bergmann (1999).

20. There is also an important advantage to my approach. On Plantinga's view, the explanation of at least some moral evil in the world is the con-

straints on God's power, and these constraints come from the truth of counterfactuals of freedom. But there doesn't seem to be any further explanation for why these counterfactuals are true. See Adams (1985, pp. 225–233). On my account, the explanation for some moral evil in the world is God's goodness, and we are helped in understanding how a good God would permit some moral evil by analogy with how good human beings would permit moral evil in comparable circumstances. In this way, I think we can have a more satisfying explanation of the compatibility of the existence of God with some moral evil in cases covered by what I call Noninterference (NI).

21. Imagine you are certain that your friend will come back to you later after he gets over his temporary depression and profusely thank you for not being fully honest with him in these circumstances.

22. Notice that while the human agents act as they do in these cases, partly because of limitations of power, God's permissive acts are simply to achieve some good.

23. It should be noted that the freedoms of wrongdoers are not always significant moral goods. Sometimes the freedoms of wrongdoers are freedoms they should not have, and clearly in such cases, these freedoms are not significant moral goods.

24. It is clear that the idea that God would, or should, be continuing intervening in human affairs to secure the more important freedoms of would-be victims at the expense of the less significant freedoms of would-be wrongdoers clearly is not part of Plantinga's Free-Will Defense.

25. The connections with freedom as noninterference still obtain if one rejects contra-causal-freedom in favor of compatibilist freedom.

26. For this conception of freedom, see Descartes (1989) and Albritton (1985).

27. It should be pointed out that any greater moral good that would serve as a justification here must also have freedom as one of its components because that is the way all moral goods are constituted for us.

Bibliography

Adams, Robert Merrihew. 1999. *Finite and Infinite Goods: A Framework for Ethics*. New York: Oxford University Press.

Adams, Marilyn. 2006. *Christ and Horrors*. New York: Cambridge University Press.

Albritton, Rogers. 1985. Freedom of Will and Freedom of Action. *Proceedings and Addresses of the American Philosophical Association* 59: 239–251.

Bergmann, Michael. 1999. Might-Counterfactuals, Transworld Untrustworthiness and Plantinga's Free Will Defense. *Faith and Philosophy* 16: 336–351.

Descartes, Rene. 1989. *Passions of the Soul Translated by Stephen Voss.* Indianapolis: Hackett Publishing Co.

Howard-Snyder, Daniel. 2013. The Logical Problem of Evil. In *The Blackwell Companion to The Problem of Evil*, ed. Justin McBrayer and Daniel Howard-Snyder. Malden: John Wiley and Sons.

Howard-Snyder, Daniel, and John O'Leary-Hawthorne. 1998. Transworld Sanctity and Plantinga's Free Will Defense. *International Journal for Philosophy of Religion* 44: 1–21.

Jimenez, Stephen. 2013. *The Book of Matt: Hidden Truths About the Murder of Matthew Shepard.* New York: Penguin/Random House.

Machan, Tibor. 2006. *Libertarianism Defended.* Burlington: Ashgate.

Mack, Eric. 1991. Libertarianism Untamed. *Journal of Social Philosophy* 22: 64–72.

Morris, Tom, and Matt Morris. 2005. *Superheroes and Philosophy: Truth, Justice and the Socratic Way.* Peru: Open Court.

Narveson, Jan. 2001. *Libertarian Idea.* Peterborough: Broadview Press.

Oropeza, B.J. 2008. *The Gospel According to Superheroes.* New York: Peter Lang.

Otte, Richard. 2009. Transworld Depravity and Unobtainable Worlds. *Philosophy and Phenomenological Research* 78: 165–177.

Plantinga, Alvin. 1974. *God, Freedom, and Evil.* New York: Harper & Row.

Pruss, Alexander. 2012. A Counterexample to Plantinga's Free Will Defense. *Faith and Philosophy* 29: 400–415.

Shepard, Judy. 2009. *The Meaning of Matthew: My Son's Murder in Laramie and a World Transformed.* New York: Hudson St. Press.

Smart, J.J.C., and J.J. Haldane. 2002. *Atheism and Theism.* 2nd ed. Malden: Blackwell.

Stengler, Victor. 2007. *God: The Failed Hypothesis.* Amherst: Prometheus.

Sterba, James P. 2014. *From Rationality to Equality.* Oxford: Oxford University Press.

3

An Attempt at Theodicy

We have seen from the previous chapter that God's permission of significant and especially horrendous evil consequences of immoral actions in the world cannot be justified by the significant freedom in it. This is because the permission of significant and especially horrendous evil consequences of immoral actions in the world results in a net loss of significant freedom in our world. So if God is to be justified in permitting all the evil in the world, it must be for other reasons.[1] So let's now consider what those other reasons might be.[2]

I

Could it be that God's permitting all the evil in our world is justified by the opportunity for soul-making it provides? Not if having the opportunity for significant soul-making in our world is dependent on having significant freedom such that a net loss of significant freedom in our world would result in a net loss of the opportunity for significant soul-making as well. Unfortunately, this does seem to be the case. Moreover, whenever serious assaults occur, what happens is that the particular

© The Author(s) 2019
J. P. Sterba, *Is a Good God Logically Possible?*,
https://doi.org/10.1007/978-3-030-05469-4_3

opportunity for soul-making of the assaulters, an opportunity for soul-making that no one ideally needs to have, is exercised badly at the expense of the opportunity for soul-making of their victims, an opportunity for soul-making that all would-be victims should have.

Could it be then that God's permitting all the evil in our world is justified by the freedom and soul-making it provides, not in this life, but in a heavenly afterlife? Not in the traditional view if freedom and soul-making requires the possibility of acting immorally. This is because in the traditional view it is assumed that people in the heavenly afterlife cannot act immorally.[3] Even in the nontraditional view of an afterlife that I defended elsewhere, where people can still act immorally in an afterlife, this proposed justification would not be available.[4] This is because in my account, people would already have all the freedom and opportunity for soul-making that they could justifiably possess in an afterlife, which they would have in their own right and not because of God's permission of all the evil in the world. So providing them with even more freedom and opportunity for soul-making would not be justified in my version of an afterlife because it would violate the rights of others to significant freedom and the significant opportunity for soul-making that goes with it.

What then about God simply conferring moral virtues on those entering the heavenly afterlife if significant evils deprived them of the opportunity for soul-making in this life?[5] But what need would people in the traditional heavenly afterlife have for moral virtues if no one can act immorally in that afterlife? Of course, in my alternative afterlife, people can still act immorally, but given that God would be preventing significant and especially horrendous consequences of immoral actions in this afterlife, further intervention would unnecessarily interfere with people's opportunity to acquire moral virtues, and hence would be unjustified.

What then could God give those deprived of the opportunities for soul-making in this life? Well, God could give them what we could call them, in contrast to the goods we have just considered, consumer goods, that is, experiences and activities that are intensely pleasurable, completely fulfilling, and all encompassing. Surely the beatific vision, which is said to involve ultimate communion or friendship with God, would presumably be the primary consumer good that would be experienced and enjoyed by those in the traditional heavenly afterlife.[6]

II

Yet in order for God to provide those who have experienced significant evils in this life with such consumer goods in a heavenly afterlife, providing those goods would have to constitute an appropriate response to individuals who have been so deprived. The problem is that the goods and evils involved seem unrelated. Why should someone deprived of the opportunities for soul-making simply be provided with the goods that only a good performance at soul-making is standardly thought to render the person less unworthy of receiving?[7] How is it fitting or appropriate to just skip the intervening step of soul-making? Imagine a runner who is unfairly kept from competing in a race. Surely, the appropriate response is not to reward the runner with a prize for performing well in the race, but rather to provide her a chance to compete in a comparable race.[8] Marilyn Adams has argued that there should be an organic unity between the evils one suffers in this life and the goods one experiences in a heavenly afterlife.[9] Yet there seems to be no organic unity at all between a person's experience of significant evils in this life, unchosen and unaccepted, and the person's being simply provided with consumer goods by God in an afterlife.

III

Nevertheless, maybe there is a way of showing how persons who suffer from the consequences of significantly evil actions in this life could be appropriately provided with the fantastic consumer goods of a heavenly afterlife. Notice that we often accept suffering in this life, or even embrace it, as a means to achieving some good. Moreover, the central message of Christianity is that Jesus Christ suffered and died on the cross to redeem us all from our sins. Even so, God presumably could have chosen different means to redeem us. Jesus's suffering and death is simply understood to be the means that God chose and that Jesus accepted for our redemption. Of course, it is true of Jesus and of individuals who experienced significant evils, unchosen and unaccepted, that they both suffered, but their experiences of suffering are radically different. Jesus's suffering was accepted by him as a way of redeeming us all. By contrast, the suffering of those deprived of the opportunities for soul-making is neither chosen nor accepted as part of any action in which the sufferers are engaged. Of course, it is possible that individuals looking back over the course of their lives from the perspective of an afterlife and seeing their unchosen and unaccepted experience of significant evils followed immediately by the fantastic consumer goods of a heavenly afterlife could still be happy with how their lives have turned out. For example, a freed slave who experienced a horrible life as a slave might still be happy to have discovered a pot of gold that enabled her to go somewhere and peacefully live out the remainder of her days. However, this sort of response would not suffice to show that the two parts of her life were organically related to each other, as Adams claims would be required in order for God to justifiably permit those evils.[10]

IV

To try to convey the organic unity that Adams thinks is required, she gives us an example of two soldiers (Ralph and Sam) who were buddies in the trenches in World War I and afterward remained life-long best friends. She says of them:

> Ralph and Sam would not have enlisted had they known in advance how bad it would be. They would never want to go through such horrors again. But because their experience in the trenches has been caught up into one of the valuable human relationships, they do not retrospectively wish it away from their lives. (Adams 2013, p. 20)

Yet what exactly are we to imagine here? Are we to imagine that Ralph and Sam have come through the war deeply scarred by its effects, as would be the case if Ralph had been left blind by the war and Sam a quadriplegic? Assume that subsequently they both lived together in a military hospital where their friendship continued. If such were the lives that Ralph and Sam were left with by the war, might they not be willing to wish away the good of their friendship if that would also remove from their lives the physical disabilities that resulted from the war as well?

Of course, Adams is probably not imagining Ralph's and Sam's lives turning out in the way I just imagined. Most likely, in her account, Ralph and Sam bear only a few scars from the war. She is probably thinking of them emerging from war relatively unscathed themselves, both physically and emotionally, but with their deep friendship a welcomed benefit of the war.

Yet even this reading of Adams's example does not support the conclusion she wants to draw. It all depends on what is implied by Ralph's and Sam's wishing their friendship away. If wishing their friendship away also involves wishing away some of the calamities brought about by the war in which they were involved, then, depending on the kind of war in which they were involved, Ralph and Sam may be willing to wish away, and actually should wish away, their friendship as well. World War I, in particular, was a devastatingly immoral war. Almost anyone who benefited from that war should be willing, morally speaking, to wish away any benefit derived from it, if that also involved wishing away some of the calamities of the war that went with it.

In light of these considerations, Adams needs to revise her example and not have Ralph and Sam be survivors of World War I, but rather have them fighting on the right side of a just war, maybe fighting for the allies in a justified part of World War II. Suppose, then, in this context, they fought bravely in the same combat unit and came to know and rely on each other on a daily basis. Then it would be the case that both of them had good reason not to wish away their wartime friendship. Even though their friendship did develop through their contributions to a military effort, we are imagining that they were fighting in a just war or in a just segment of a war, so that the harms they imposed on others would have been morally justified. In such a context, their friendship would be a welcomed side-effect of their involvement in a justified war effort. So now we have a case where Ralph and Sam's wartime friendship develops out of their participation in a just war or in a just segment of a war. In fact, it is the evils of war in which Ralph and Sam were engaged that made their friendship possible.[11]

V

However, there seems to be no similarity between the relationship that exists between wartime friendships and the evils of warfare and the relationship that exists between a heavenly afterlife and significant evils that are unchosen and unwanted beyond the fact that in both cases we find a good related to an evil.

Nevertheless, Adams wants to see more similarity between the cases than that. For her, victims of significant evils are really like soldiers who become fast friends in foxholes and who would not retrospectively wish away their friendships. She says that

> from the vantage point of heaven, when they recognize how God was with them in their worst experience, [they] will not wish to eliminate any moments of intimacy with God from their life histories. (Adams 2006, p. 40)

Yet how would knowing retrospectively that God was standing by, so to speak, as one endured significant suffering, lead one, in retrospect, not to wish that any of that suffering be eliminated? The person's suffering is clearly unrelated to the heavenly afterlife she is now experiencing. The sufferer did not choose or accept that suffering for any good purpose that would have made her less unworthy of the heavenly afterlife she is now experiencing. That suffering was simply inflicted on her against her will and then was followed immediately after her death with a heavenly afterlife. And now we are to imagine that persons, who had suffered so intensely, looking back on their experience from the perspective of their heavenly afterlives, somehow being unwilling to wish away that suffering because they know, what they didn't know at the time, that God was standing there, so to speak, throughout their entire ordeals, although not intervening in any way to lessen their suffering. Yet why should that new knowledge now reconcile a person to her horrible experience and make her not want to wish it away even in retrospect? Just knowing retrospectively that God was there, standing by, so to speak, does not appear to make the person's suffering organically related to a heavenly reward. Imagining that God is there would imply that the joining of the two things together was God's will, but the mere fact that God wills two things to go together is not enough to make the two things organically related to each other.[12] For example, our two soldiers, Ralph and Sam, might also come to see from the perspective of a heavenly afterlife that God too was there for them, standing by, so to speak, as they fought side by side in a just segment of the war in which they were engaged. Yet knowing retrospectively of God's presence would not be what made the good of their friendship organically related to the evils of the war in which they participated, thereby justifying their participation in those evils. The organic unity of Adams's example is clearly unrelated to any retrospective knowledge of God's presence, which can easily be included in our understanding of the example without affecting our assessment of its organic unity, one way or the other.[13]

VI

Now it might be useful here to compare the way that the good of wartime friendships relate to the evil of war with the way that the good of a heavenly afterlife relates to suffering or evil in this life. Clearly, it is morally acceptable not to want to wish away a wartime friendship when that friendship emerged from fighting on the right side of a just war or in a just segment of a war. At the same time, it would be morally unacceptable for us not to want to wish away a wartime friendship when that friendship emerged from fighting on the wrong side of a just war or in an unjust segment of a war, especially when wishing it away would also involve wishing away some of the wartime calamities during which the friendship was formed. In the latter case, we can, of course, recognize that there might be self-interested reasons to act immorally and to remain involved in the unjust war or unjust segment of a war from which the friendship emerged, at the same time that we recognize that this is a case where morality definitely trumps self-interest rather than accords with it.

Similarly, it is morally acceptable not to want to wish away a heavenly afterlife when, through a process of soul-making, people have done what they can to make themselves less unworthy of such a life. At the same time, it would be morally unacceptable not to want to wish away a heavenly afterlife if it turned out that one had no more basis for receiving such a life than the experience of significant evils, unchosen and unaccepted.[14] In this case, we can, of course, recognize that there would be strong self-interested reasons not to want to wish away such a heavenly afterlife. Nevertheless, we can also recognize that it is morally inappropriate to receive such a heavenly afterlife on such a basis when others have received it only after they have done their best to make themselves less unworthy candidates for receiving it.

So in the end, Adams turns out to be right about the analogy between victims of horrors and soldiers in warfare, once that comparison is properly drawn. Thus, just as soldiers should be willing to wish away their wartime friendships when they have not developed through fighting in a just war or in a just segment of a war, victims of significant evils should be willing to wish away a heavenly reward as morally inappropriate for them when they have done nothing to make themselves less unworthy candidates for receiving it.

Rather, what would appear to be morally appropriate for all those who have been denied the significant freedoms necessary for soul-making is for them to be placed in a second-inning afterlife where they would have the opportunity, through soul-making, to make themselves less unworthy for receiving a heavenly afterlife.[15]

VII

Interestingly, Adams too sees the need for a corrective in the afterlife. She says:

> Many participants in horrors do not recognize or appropriate the positive meanings of their lives…before they die. Therefore, if such individuals are to have lives that are great goods to them on the whole, God must be able to preserve them in life after their death, to place them … in a new and nourishing environment where they can profit from Divine instruction on how to integrate their participation in horrors into wholes with positive meanings. (Adams 1999, pp. 83–4)

Accordingly, Adams thinks that an afterlife is needed to make clear to these victims how their experience of significant evils fits into their lives in an integrated way so as to make their lives great goods for them as a whole. She thinks that can be done by linking the suffering of these victims to the redemptive suffering of Jesus. However, I have argued that the sufferings of these victims, which are unchosen and unaccepted, cannot be linked to the sufferings of Jesus, which was both chosen and accepted. You just cannot take something that was unchosen and unaccepted and make it part of something an agent does that works to her overall good.

Adams tries to get around this problem by interpreting the victims of significant evils to be choosing their suffering retrospectively from the perspective of a heavenly afterlife. But I have argued that people cannot really accept their suffering from that standpoint so as to make it part of their overall good. Rather, from that standpoint, people would see the moral inappropriateness of their being provided with a heavenly afterlife. What they would want is a second-inning afterlife that gives them the significant freedoms required for the soul-making that would enable them to make themselves into less unworthy candidates for a heavenly afterlife.

VIII

Still, there are problems with this idea of a second-inning afterlife. Here we are imagining people having the same options for soul-making that they would have had in this life had God not allowed them to experience significant evils in this life that took away those opportunities from them. Unfortunately, such second-inning afterlives could seemingly give rise to significant evils of their own, leading to a need for third-inning afterlives, and on and on.

Another problem is whether to understand each n-inning afterlife as continuous in some sense with the person's previous life or lives. On the one hand, if it is not continuous at all, and entering such an afterlife is like starting life all over again, that makes the horrendous evils in the person's previous life or lives just look like a big mistake on God's part from the victim's point of view. Victims would get no benefit from the significant evils they experience in their previous lives, save the chance to start all over again, although without any knowledge that they are, in fact, doing so.[16]

On the other hand, if an n-inning life were somewhat continuous with a person's past, people could bring with them some, but, of course, not all the effects (since some were deadly) of the significant evils in their previous lives, as well as other characteristics of their previous lives. But does this mean that the social contexts of their second-inning lives would be something like the social contexts of their previous lives? If so, where would the people living together in these n-inning afterlives come from? Presumably, they would all be people who were in need of one or more afterlives. But then all the inhabitants of these n-inning afterlives would be in worlds similar yet still strangely different from the worlds in which they had lived their previous lives. They would realize that in their afterlives, their social environments had changed in the direction of providing them with the significant freedom necessary for soul-making that they had lacked in their previous lives. They most surely would recognize a providential influence in their lives that is probably far greater than anything God would have had to do in this life to prevent the experience of significant evils from denying people of the freedom they required for soul-making. Clearly, this appears to be a more convoluted way of producing basically the same outcome that could have been produced in this life had God simply prevented wrongdoers from taking away the significant freedoms that people required for soul-making in this life. Without a doubt, then, the important question that remains is whether an omni-God really has this option? Put another way, is there some overriding moral objection to God's dealing with significant evils in this way?

In the next chapter, I take up the question of whether there is an overriding moral objection to God's dealing with significant evils in this way. In both traditional and contemporary ethics, there is a moral principle that seems to be in direct conflict with God's permitting evil and then making up for it later. That moral principle, embedded in the Doctrine of Double Effect, is frequently referred to as the Pauline Principle because it was endorsed by St. Paul (Romans 3:8). The principle holds that we should never do evil that good may come of it. It has been a mainstay of natural law ethics at least since the time of Aquinas.[17] Unfortunately, it has tended to be ignored by contemporary philosophers of religion when discussing the problem of evil. In the next chapter, I hope to begin to supply the discussion that is needed.

Notes

1. It is worth noting that the course of argument we are pursuing here is available only to a deontologist who thinks that there are exceptions to the requirement never to do or permit evil that good may come of it or that sometimes the end does justify the means. An absolute deontologist would summarily reject this line of argument and therefore would immediately be led to the conclusion that God does not exist. Here I am assuming that the absolute deontologist is mistaken about this. Later, however, I will base my argument on specific moral requirements that are acceptable to both consequentialist and deontologists alike, including absolute deontologists.
2. I am assuming here that a morally good God would not arbitrarily assign just some people to a heavenly afterlife, and that where people ended up would appropriately depends to some extent on what they did and/or chose to believe.
3. It might be objected that if we could still be free in a heavenly afterlife without the possibility of acting immorally, why can't we be free in the same way in this life? That would mean that there would be no moral evil in this life just as there is said to be no moral evil in the traditional heavenly afterlife. The usual response to this objection is that creatures, like ourselves, could only be appropriately free in the afterlife if we first have proved ourselves through soul-making in this life, where we had the possibility of acting immorally. This response also shows why those who have been deprived of the significant freedom required for soul-making in this life cannot be candidates for admission to the heavenly afterlife until they too have proven themselves, after having been provided with the freedom necessary for soul-making. This idea that people must show themselves at least less unworthy of a heavenly afterlife through a process of soul-making before being able to enter into a heavenly afterlife is surely a morally defensible element to theism. This, of course, holds for those who are capable, given the opportunity, of doing what we could be reasonably expected to do to make themselves less unworthy of such a

life through soul-making. For those who lack such a capacity something else may be morally appropriate.

Nevertheless, it is possible that God could have made creatures different from us, who are free without the possibility of acting immorally in the way that God is said to be free yet can never act immorally. Of course, God would be under no obligation to anyone to make a world with such creatures rather than a world with creatures, like ourselves, whose freedom in this life is such that we can and sometimes do act immorally. The only obligation God would have is to create creatures whose lives are worth living (otherwise they would be better off never existing!), and to take care of whatever creatures he decides to create. Nothing else is morally required.

4. See Sterba (2018).

5. Whenever I speak in this chapter of significant evils, I am here restricting the class to those evils that are caused by human actions, not simply by natural forces.

6. For an account of the beatific vision, see Aquinas (1947, III, Q 9, a2 obj. 3).

7. There is a general problem here. Why should a heavenly afterlife be an appropriate response to soul-making or living a morally good life? Moral actions when properly motivated are done because they are the right thing to do not because they lead to anything like a reward, heavenly or otherwise. Of course, in some cases, particularly with regard to self-regarding virtues, like temperance, the right thing to do is truly good for oneself. However, what would be bad is for immoral people to benefit from their wrongdoing. So what is required is not that virtuous people be rewarded for their virtue and bad people punished for their vice, but rather that people, both the morally good and the morally bad, get what they deserve. Thus, what morally good people deserve is not necessarily a reward, unless they are in a contest and then they desire the reward not for being morally good, per se, but rather for being the best contestant in the contest. So when we say that it is appropriate for morally good people to have a heavenly reward, it cannot be because they deserve it as a reward for being moral. So maybe the idea is that if anyone is going to get a heavenly afterlife, better that it goes to those who have made themselves, as far as possible, the least unworthy of receiving it, and morally good people are clearly less unworthy than others to receive a heavenly afterlife. Alternatively, we could construe at least part of the required

soul-making to include pursuing a friendship with God because that clearly would be relevant to how unworthy one would be to entering a heavenly afterlife.

8. Even while I am using the imagery of running in a race, I don't want to prejudge whether what is required of the to-be-blessed is some special kind of good works rather than some special kind of faith. Even so, I tend to think that what is involved, the "special kind" in each case, incorporates some of what we normally mean by both faith and good works taken together. Moreover, by faith here I mean belief that goes beyond not against reason, so it must be consistent with what reason tells us.

9. In an organic unit, the value of the components taken together is greater than the value of the sum of those components taken separately.

10. In addition, as I have argued, it would be morally inappropriate for God to bestow the fantastic consumer good of a heavenly afterlife without any connection to what a person did or chose to believe.

11. Notice that I am allowing that in all these combat friendships an organic unity can develop between such friendships and particular wars or segments of wars, even though the participants should be willing to wish those friendships away because they developed through an unjust war or an unjust segment of a war. So, in fact, that an organic relationship exists between two things is clearly not enough to morally justify them. However, an organic unity can be a necessary requirement for moral justification in certain cases, as Adams suggests.

12. Adams seems to be suggesting that knowledge that God is present when the two things are connected suffices to show that there is an organic connection between those two things. But if this is the basis for an organic connection, then it is trivially true that such connections would be present wherever two things are connected because God, on the standard view, is present everywhere. But I do not think that Adams is holding such a trivial thesis.

13. There is an interesting difference between the way that Adams treats the wartime-friendship/evils-of-war example and the significant-evils/heavenly afterlife example. In the first case, she wants us to consider whether we would wish away the good (the wartime friendship). In the second case, she wants us to consider whether we would wish away the evil (the horrendous evils, unchosen and unaccepted). In my final treatment of the two examples, I take it to be most relevant to just ask about wishing away the good in each case.

14. Although living a morally good life and engaging in soul-making will not make someone deserving a heavenly life (or even make one worthy of it), having done none of these things certainly makes receiving a heavenly life morally inappropriate.

15. Note that one can, at least in part, make oneself a less unworthy candidate for being provided with a heavenly afterlife by doing one's best to establish and maintain morally good and just relationships with one's fellow human beings without making it the case that one ever deserves or is worthy of that heavenly afterlife.

16. Adams strongly objects to this interpretation of a second-inning afterlife.

17. See, for example, the fundamental role it plays in the contemporary natural law ethics of John Finnis.

Bibliography

Adams, Marilyn. 1999. Horrendous Evils. Ithaca: Cornell University Press.
———. 2006. *Christ and Horrors*. New York: Cambridge University Press.
———. 2013. Ignorance, Instrumentality, Compensation and the Problem of Evil. *Sophia* 52: 7–26.
Aquinas, Thomas 1947. *Summa Theologiae*. Trans. The Fathers of the English Dominican Province. New York: Benziger Brother Inc.
Sterba, James P. 2018. Eliminating the Problem of Hell. *Religious Studies*.

4

The Pauline Principle and the Just Political State

In both traditional and contemporary ethics we find an ethical principle that seems to be in direct conflict with God's permitting evil and then making up for it later.[1] That ethical principle is embedded in the Doctrine of Double Effect and frequently referred to as the Pauline Principle because it was endorsed by St. Paul (Romans 3:8). The principle holds that we should never do evil that good may come of it.

Now it is true that the Pauline Principle has been rejected as an absolute principle. This is because there clearly seem to be exceptions to it. Surely doing evil that good may come of it is justified when the resulting evil or harm is:

1. trivial (e.g., as in the case of stepping on someone's foot to get out of a crowded subway) or
2. easily reparable (e.g., as in the case of lying to a temporarily depressed friend to keep him from committing suicide).

There is also disagreement over whether a further exception to the principle obtains when the resulting evil or harm is:

© The Author(s) 2019
J. P. Sterba, *Is a Good God Logically Possible?*,
https://doi.org/10.1007/978-3-030-05469-4_4

3. the only way to prevent a far greater harm to innocent people (e.g., as in the case of shooting one of twenty civilian hostages to prevent, in the only way possible, the execution of all twenty).

Yet despite the belief that there are exceptions to the principle, and despite the disagreement over the extent of those exceptions, the Pauline Principle still plays an important role in ethical theory.

Moreover, the widespread discussion of hypothetical trolley cases in contemporary ethical theory is frequently just another way of determining the range of application of the Pauline Principle. There is then an intertwining discussion of trolley cases with the Pauline Principle which underlies the Doctrine of Double Effect in contemporary ethical theory that is ignored by contemporary philosophers of religion when they seek to morally evaluate the problem of evil.

Nevertheless, given that there are standard exceptions to the Pauline Principle, might not God's permission of evil fall under them? Well, consider how morally constrained these standard exceptions to the Pauline Principle are. They allow us to do evil that good may come of it only when the evil is trivial, easily reparable, or the only way to prevent a far greater harm to innocents. So it is difficult to see how God's widespread permission of the harmful consequences of significantly evil actions could be a justified exception to the Pauline Principle.

In addition, the standard exceptions that are allowed only seem to be allowed because the agents involved lack the power to accomplish the good or avoid the evil in any other way. Lack of power is crucially important to the justification of these exceptions. Yet clearly God is not subject to any such limitation of power. Thus, God can negotiate crowded subways without harming anyone in the slightest. God can also prevent a temporarily depressed person from committing suicide without lying to them, and God can save all twenty civilian hostages without having to execute any one of them. Consequently, none of these exceptions to the Pauline Principle that are permitted to agents, like ourselves, because of our limited power, would hold for God.

I

Nevertheless, there may be a broader range of exceptions to the Pauline Principle. To see this, consider the analogy of a political state that is aiming to secure a significant degree of justice for its members. Such a state would not try to prevent all the moral evil that occurs in its domain, even if that were within its power to do so. Instead, a just state would focus on preventing significant and especially horrendous moral evils that impact people's lives. It would not seek to prevent lesser evils because any general attempt to prevent such evils would tend to interfere with people's significant freedoms.[2] Rather, a just state would leave such evils to be used by individuals for soul-making as far as possible. Similarly, God, like a just state, should be focused on preventing (not permitting) just the consequences of significant and especially horrendous moral evils which impact on people's lives, thus leaving wrongdoers the freedom to imagine, intend, and even to take initial steps toward carrying out their wrongdoing in such cases.

Now it might be objected here that while God cannot do evil that good may come of it, God could permit evil that good may come of it. Of course, moral philosophers do recognize a distinction between doing and permitting evil. Doing evil is normally worse than permitting evil. But when the evil is significant and one can easily prevent it, then permitting evil can become morally equivalent to doing it. The same kind of moral blame attaches to both actions. Think of someone who permitted a family member to be brutally raped. Surely the "permitting" here has the same moral status as a "doing." Likewise, God's permitting significantly evil consequences when those consequences can easily be prevented is morally equivalent to God's doing something that is seriously wrong.

It might also be objected that God is not really intending evil consequences at all but merely foreseeing their occurrence, or, put another way, God is intentionally doing something, that is, making us free, but then God is only foreseeing the evil consequences that result therefrom.[3] Yet God is said to be permitting those evil consequences, and permitting is an intentional act. So if God intends not to stop the evil consequences of our actions when he can easily do so then he is not merely foreseeing those consequences.[4]

Now the permitting of evils that do not interfere with people's signifi-cant freedom could be taken to be justified exceptions to the Pauline Principle's prohibition on the doing and permitting of evil for God and ourselves. However, we might not want to interpret as exceptions to the Pauline Principle the acts of failing to prevent evils that do not interfere with people's significant freedom, especially when such evils can also be used by individuals for soul-making. We might not consider "these fail-ings to prevent evil" to be important enough to rise to the level of actions that should be prohibited by the Pauline Principle. In which case, these failings to prevent evil would still be justified; they would just not be justified as exceptions to the Pauline Principle. Surely, this is a viable interpretation. Yet there is a theoretical advantage to viewing all actions that are wrong in themselves, even such trivial actions as intentionally stepping on someone's foot to get out of a crowded subway, as violations of the Pauline Principle, but then overridable because the basic interests of the person harmed are not affected. Still, what remains the case is that both for a just political state and for God, the prevention of evils that do interfere with people's significant freedom is required by the Pauline Principle, and this requirement applies even more strongly to God than it does to a just political state.

II

It is sometimes argued that if God were actually engaged in preventing significant and especially horrendous evil consequences, the world we would be living in would not have the real freedom that is required for soul-making. Accordingly, it is argued that if God were so engaged in preventing evil, we would just be left with what has been called "toy free-dom" by a theist (Richard Swinburne) or "playpen freedom" by an atheist (David Lewis) and that would greatly diminish our status as moral agents.[5]

Now no one doubts that there would be a problem if God always intervened to prevent evil. If that were to happen, then the freedom we would be left with would hardly be worthy of the name. Clearly, we must have the freedom to do wrong if we are to develop through soul-making the virtue that would make ourselves less unworthy of a heavenly afterlife. But having the freedom needed for soul-making is not the same as having unlimited freedom. A world where everyone has unlimited freedom is not an ideal world by any stretch of the imagination. Rather, such a world could easily become a war of all against all, or a war of the thugs against the rest. By contrast, what would be ideal from the perspective of freedom is a world where everyone's freedom is appropriately constrained. Toy freedom or a playpen freedom is a problem only where freedom is constrained too much, not where it is appropriately constrained. But when are constraints on freedom too much and when are they appropriate?

III

In Chap. 2, I argued that the freedoms that victims lose by the serious wrongdoings of others are much more important than the freedoms that are exercised by those who wrong them. I claimed that there is a net loss of significant freedom whenever such wrongdoing occurs and there is no way that this net loss of freedom can be made up for by freedom that is logically connected to this permission. Accordingly, I contend that if we want to appropriately constrain freedom, we should have a policy that constrains the less significant freedoms of would-be wrongdoers in order to secure the more significant freedoms of their would-be victims. Surely, that would be a justified policy of constraint. In addition, it would not deprive would-be wrongdoers of their status as moral agents nor would it leave them with only a toy or a playpen freedom. Thus, even when serious wrongdoers are prevented from carrying out the final steps of their evil actions with significant and especially horrendous consequences for their victims, they would still have the freedom to imagine, intend, and even take initial steps toward carrying out their wrongdoing.

Nevertheless, it might be objected that if God did get involved in preventing significant and especially horrendous evil consequences of immoral acts, people would just stop imagining, intending, or even taking the initial steps toward carrying out such actions. God's constraining interventions with respect to the consequences of significantly and especially horrendously evil actions would, in effect, put a stop to anyone's later engaging in the initial stages of any such evil deeds as well. So we would be left with only toy or playpen freedom after all.

Michael Murray gives a useful example that appears to support this conclusion. Murray reports:

> When I was five years old, I and a few other boys at Towpath Elementary School decided that we wanted to fly. At recess we assembled at the top of the concrete wall at the edge of the playground. One after another we jumped off the wall, flapping our arms as hard as we could, each crashing to the ground in disappointment. Of course, as the first few plopped to the ground, some of those still to jump were convinced that those who failed to fly failed only out of lack of strength or skill. But after twenty minutes of consistent failure and sore behinds we all decided that flying was not in our future. To the best of my knowledge, no one in that group has since been tempted to fly off a concrete wall. Indeed, I suspect none of my kindergarten companions could now even form the intention to fly off the wall. They all know by their experience that doing so is as impossible as leaping to the moon or swallowing the ocean. (Murray 2008, p. 137)

And so Murray concludes:

> If God were simply to block the evil consequences of our actions, choosing evil would be no more possible for us than choosing to fly or choosing to jump to the moon is for us in the actual world. (Ibid.)

The problem with Murray's use of this example is that he overgeneralizes from it. Surely, the disastrous experience of the kindergarteners deterred them from even trying or intending to try to do again exactly what they tried to do on that occasion. Yet even the kindergarteners, later, possibly when grown up, could go on to try to accomplish analogous feats, maybe this time attaching gliders to their arms and attempting to fly from a much higher elevation with a stiff wind at their backs. Similarly, significant evil is not just the result of one specific action, such that if one is unsuccessful at producing that action's evil consequences, then one is quickly going to conclude that one will be unsuccessful at doing anything even remotely similar to that action on other occasions. Certainly, that is

not the pattern played out in fictional accounts of superheroes and ordinary villains. Instead, after their evil plans have been frustrated by a
superhero on one occasion, these villains do not give up on villainy alto-
gether. Rather, they strive to find some other occasion, or some other set
of circumstances, where they can still succeed at their villainy.

Furthermore, we are not imagining that God is always preventing the
evil consequences of wrongful actions. Rather, we are assuming that God
would be allowing evildoers to bring about the evil consequences of their
actions for a broad range of cases where the consequences, especially for
others, are not significantly evil. We are also assuming that God would be
allowing would-be wrongdoers to imagine, intend, or even take the initial steps toward carrying out their seriously wrongful actions, and just
stopping wrongdoers from bringing about significantly and especially
horrendously evil consequences of those actions.[6] Hence, all of these
imaginings, intendings, taking initial steps, and actually realizing the
consequences of one's actions should provide ample training ground for
soul-making.

An imperfect analogy of what God should be doing here is provided in
the film *Minority Report* starring Tom Cruise in which information from
psychics that murders were about to be committed is used by a "PreCrime"
division of a D.C./Northern Virginia police department to apprehend
would-be murderers before they can commit their murders. In the film,
the detection system is misused by its originator and is eventually shut
down. But such misuse would never occur if God were operating on the
basis of the knowledge that is presumably available to him about the
consequences of our actions. A more real-life analogy of what God should
be doing is provided by the US Department of Homeland Security's
Future Attribute Screening Technology (FAST) program, currently under
development. FAST uses noncontact sensors to remotely analyze physi-
ological/behavior patterns including pupil dilation, breathing, facial
expression, and other such factors that an individual does not consciously
control. The system then conducts a real-time analysis of the data col-
lected and then transmits recommendations back to on-site screeners.
The Department of Homeland Security claims that FAST has recently
demonstrated 70–74% accuracy when using only remote, noncontact
sensors; earlier testing demonstrated up to 81% accuracy when using

contact sensors.[7] Of course, imperfect accuracy and the false-positives problem inherent in such screening would not be present if God were engaged in just preventing significant and especially horrendous consequences of our wrongful actions.

IV

Here it is important to push a bit further the analogy of God acting like a just political state. Clearly, such a state would be interested not only in preventing interferences with the significant freedom of its members but also with promoting significant freedom for its members. God, then, like a just state, would presumably have similar interests. So God should be interested in preventing interferences with the significant freedom of would-be victims by wrongdoers as well as with promoting significant freedom where possible. Nevertheless, there are important differences between ourselves and God in this regard relating to the Pauline Principle.

Now the Pauline Principle prohibits doing evil that good may come of it. But good can come of evil in two ways. It can come by way of *preventing evil* or it can come by way of *providing some new good*.[8] For us, all the serious exceptions to the Pauline Principle are of the first type. Recall the extreme case given earlier of shooting one of twenty civilian hostages to prevent, in the only way possible, the execution of all twenty. In that case, the evil is clearly done to prevent a much more significant evil.[9]

Here it is very important to notice that God is always in a position to prevent such significant evil from happening by simply withdrawing his permissive will without having to violate the Pauline Principle to do so. In all such cases, God's intervention would restrict a not very important freedom of would-be wrongdoers in order to secure significant freedoms for those who would otherwise be victims. Surely, that would be the best way to bring about a morally defensible distribution of freedom in such cases. It also has the additional desirable feature of not in any way coming into conflict with the Pauline Principle. So in contexts where what is at issue is whether to permit significant evil to prevent a greater evil, it would never be morally permissible for God to permit either evil because

God would always be able to prevent both evils in such cases. So in contexts where what is at issue is whether to do or permit significant lesser evil to prevent a greater evil, it would never be morally permissible for God to permit significant lesser evil because God would always be able to prevent the greater evil without permitting the lesser evil unless there is also a significant good that would justify God in permitting the lesser evil to provide that good.

So then let's consider the second type of case where God's permitting a significant evil is the means to provide some significant good rather than to prevent some significant evil. Consider a case involving just human agents. Suppose parents you know were to permit their children to be brutally assaulted to make possible the soul-making of the person who would attempt to comfort their children after they have been assaulted or to make possible the soul-making that their children themselves could experience by coming to forgive their assailants. Would you think the parents were morally justified in so acting? Hardly. Here you surely would agree with the Pauline Principle's prohibition of such actions. Permitting one's children to be brutally assaulted is an action that is wrong in itself, and not something that could be permitted for the sake of whatever good consequences it might happen to have. That is why the Pauline Principle prohibits any appeal to good consequences to justify such actions in such cases.

So for human agents, given that such intrinsically wrongful actions would significantly conflict with the basic interests of their victims, there are no exceptions to the Pauline Principle for cases of this sort where the significant evil that is to be done is just a means to securing a good to which the beneficiary is not entitled. Moreover, if there are no exceptions to the Pauline Principle for humans in such cases, then the same should also hold true for God. If it is always wrong for us to do actions of a certain sort, then it should always be wrong for God to do them as well. So for contexts where the issue is whether to permit a significant evil to achieve some additional good, God, like us, would never be justified in permitting evil in such cases.[10]

In sum, God could not permit significant moral evil to prevent a greater moral evil because he could always prevent the greater evil without permitting the lesser evil and God, like us, could not permit significant moral evil to attain a good to which the beneficiary is not entitled because there are no exceptions to the Pauline Principle in this regard.[11] This is why the Pauline Principle raises such a serious challenge to reconciling God to the degree and amount of evil in the world.

V

Now given that God does not generally prevent significantly evil consequences of the wrongful actions we observe in our world, and, as a result, at least some of the victims of such wrongdoing are deprived of the significant freedom they require for soul-making in this life, there is a need to provide them with at least a second-inning afterlife, where they would have the significant freedom needed for soul-making. Otherwise they could never have the opportunity to engage in the virtuous behavior needed to make them less unworthy of a heavenly afterlife.[12] It would also be morally inappropriate for anyone, even after having suffered significant evils that were unchosen and unaccepted to enter the heavenly afterlife without first having gone through a soul-making that renders them less unworthy of that afterlife.[13]

Of course, there are difficulties inherent in the idea of such an afterlife, especially given that any such second-inning afterlife, without God's intervention, can lead to a need for a third-inning afterlife and on and on. It would also be difficult to give these n-inning afterlifers comparable opportunities for soul-making to those that they would have had in this life if only God had intervened in the first place to prevent the horrendous evils they experienced.[14] Moreover, unless the experience of significant evil that is unchosen and unaccepted is somehow just wiped away (thus rendering it a mistake from the victim's point of view) the experience will almost always be an alien factor in one's life, always something one is trying to overcome or put aside in order to get along with one's life, never something one could integrate into one's own good, and so not wish away if one could. Accordingly, even if n-inning afterlifers are given comparable opportunities for soul-making to the opportunities they were deprived of in this life, that would not serve to justify God's permission of the significant evils they experienced in this life and possibly in n-inning afterlives as well. Rather, it would only serve to compensate the victims of significant evils for their lost opportunities. That by itself would not suffice to justify God's failing to prevent the significant evils in the first place.[15]

VI

As we have seen, the cases where it would be justified for God not to prevent moral evil are analogous to those where it would be justified for a just political state not to prevent moral evil. Accordingly, a just political state would not try to prevent all the moral evil that occurs in its domain, even if that were within its power to do so. Instead, a just state would focus on preventing the significant moral evils that impact on people's lives. It would not seek to prevent lesser evils because any general attempt to prevent such evils would tend to interfere with people's significant freedoms.[16] Similarly, God, like a just political state, should not try to prevent every moral evil. Instead, like a just political state, God should focus on preventing the significant moral evils that impact people's lives. God should not seek to prevent lesser evils because any general attempt to prevent such evils would tend to interfere with people's significant freedoms. Accordingly, both God and a just political state should be focused on preventing the significant consequences of moral evils, making no attempt to prohibit all moral evil because that would interfere with people's significant freedom. Now the Pauline Principle and any justified exceptions to it can be interpreted to impose the same requirement: Prevent or do not permit significant moral evil but allow lesser evils whose general prohibition would interfere with people's significant freedoms.[17]

So the analogy with a just political state buttressed by the Pauline Principle shows that it is morally impermissible for God to permit the loss of significant freedom to victims of wrongdoing to prevent a greater evil given that God is required to exercise his power and prevent the greater evil without permitting the lesser evil and, just as for ourselves, it is morally impermissible for God to permit significant evil to provide some new good because there are no justified exceptions of this sort for ourselves or for God.[18]

VII

It might be objected here that if God were to act analogously to a just political state that would eliminate the need for there to be any such states. Thus suppose that you, like a just political state, had done all that you could to prevent the consequences of some significantly evil action and you could see that you were not going to be completely successful. Suppose that at that moment God were to intervene and provide what is additionally needed to completely prevent those evil consequences. Presumably, you would be pleased that God had so intervened. Now imagine you are again considering whether to intervene to prevent the consequences of another significantly evil action. You might reason that if you did intervene you might well be successful this time. Yet upon further reflection you might decide that there is really no need for you to intervene at all because if you do nothing, you could now assume that God would intervene as he had done before and this time completely prevent the significantly evil consequences from happening. So you do nothing.

According to some theists, it is just this hypothetical behavior that explains why God does not normally intervene to prevent the evil consequences of our wrongful actions. If God were to so intervene, these theists claim, people would lose the motivation they have to intervene themselves, and thereby fail to utilize the opportunities they have for soul-making. Interestingly, some atheists agree that people would no longer be motivated to intervene themselves if God normally intervened to prevent evil consequences of wrongful actions.[19] They differ in claiming that that is just what God should do. A good God, they claim, would always prevent evil consequences of wrongful actions, irrespective of whether such interventions eliminated possibilities for soul-making.

Yet both these views are wrong. It is neither the case that God should always be preventing the evil consequences of our actions nor the case that God should only rarely be preventing the evil consequences of our actions. This is because there is a third option, one that God would be morally required to take, that involves limited intervention. To see this, consider again the second case where you decided not to intervene to prevent significantly evil consequences on the assumption that God himself would completely prevent such consequences as he had helped do before. Now here, I claim, God would be morally required to intervene to prevent the evil consequences. Nevertheless, God's prevention should only be partially successful.

Here is why. Originally, let's say, you were in a position to prevent the abduction of a small boy into a car. Now that you have chosen to do nothing, you witness the abductors successfully driving off with the boy. Only later do you learn that the car was subsequently stopped by a passing patrol car because it had a busted tail-light, and the small boy, now somewhat traumatized, but otherwise unharmed, was then discovered in the car and freed by the police. So you assume, not unreasonably, that God was involved in this prevention as well as in the earlier one. Nevertheless, you cannot help but note that the intervention was not as successful as it presumably would have been if you had chosen to intervene yourself. After all, imagine that you were standing close to the boy. You could have just screamed to alert others and/or pulled the boy away and completed foiled the abductors. As a result, the boy would not have been as traumatized as he was after having been for a period of time in the hands of his abductors before the police finally rescued him.

So in this hypothetical world, you begin to detect a pattern in God's interventions. When you choose to intervene to prevent significantly evil consequences, either you will be completely successful in preventing those consequences or your intervention will fall short. When the latter is going to happen, God does something to make the prevention completely successful. Likewise, when you choose not to intervene to prevent such consequences, God again intervenes but not in a way that is fully successful. Here there is a residue of evil consequences that the victim still does suffer. This residue is not a significant evil in its own right, but it is harmful nonetheless, and it is something for which you are primarily responsible. You could have prevented those harmful consequences but you chose not to do so and that makes you responsible for them. Of course, God too could prevent those harmful consequences from happening even if you don't. It is just that in such cases God chooses not to intervene so as to completely prevent all the consequences of significantly wrongful actions in order to leave you with a limited opportunity for soul-making. Moreover, I maintain that this is exactly what God, like a just political state, and in accord with the Pauline Principle, would be required to do: Prevent the significantly evil consequences of wrongful actions, but not lesser evils so as not to interfere with people's significant freedom to use those lesser evils for soul-making as much as possible.

Yet wouldn't such a policy of limited intervention by God constrain good people from being supervirtuous at the same time that it constrains bad people from being the supervicious? If God is going to prevent the significantly evil consequences of our actions, then both good people and bad people are going to be restricted from inflicting significantly evil consequences on others. That means that good people will not be able to be as virtuous as they could otherwise be if they could freely refrain from inflicting significantly evil consequences on others. It also means that bad people will not be able to be as vicious as they could otherwise be if they could freely inflict significantly evil consequences on others.

But is this a problem? Who would object to God's following such a policy? Of course, bad people might object because such a policy limits them in the exercise of their superviciousness. But there is no reason God or anyone else should listen to their objection in this regard. What about the good people? Would they object to such a policy? How could they? True, the policy does limit good people in the exercise of their supervirtuousness, but that is just what it takes to protect would-be victims from the significantly evil consequences of the actions of bad people. Surely, good people would find the prevention of the infliction of significantly evil consequences on would-be victims by the supervicious worth the constraint imposed on how supervirtuous they themselves could be. In fact, they should find such tradeoffs not only morally acceptable but also morally required.

Consider the analogy of the criminal justice system of a just political state. Such a system would attempt to constrain bad people from being supervicious by, among other things, preventing the significantly evil consequences of their actions. But in so doing this criminal justice system would also effectively constrain morally good people from being supervirtuous by also denying them the freedom to inflict the significantly evil consequences of their actions on others. The laws and practices of the criminal justice system that constrain the supervicious from being supervicious would also constrain the supervirtuous from being supervirtuous. Yet when the supervirtuous realize that the constraints imposed on them serve to prevent the infliction of significant evil consequences on would-be victims by the supervicious, they surely would welcome those restrictions. Only the supervicious would object to the constraints, and surely morally good people would have no reason to listen to their objection. Likewise, morally good people should have no reason to object to God's following a policy of limited intervention, despite the constraint that such a policy imposes on themselves once they recognize that those constraints are just what it takes to prevent significantly evil consequences from being inflicted on would-be victims. In fact, they will surely welcome those restrictions regarding them as morally required. Only the supervicious would object to the policy of limit intervention that I have argued God should be following and clearly the supervicious have no moral grounds for doing so.

Now it might be objected that God may already be preventing the greater amount of the significant and especially the horrendous evil consequences of immoral action that would otherwise occur in our world, maybe even 99% of it, and, if so, we should not fault him for failing to prevent the remaining small percent. But clearly this is not the way we experience our world. We do not perceive that significant and especially horrendous evil consequences are being prevented virtually all of the time by Godly or by natural means. And even if our perception were grossly mistaken here, God should still be preventing the remaining significant and especially horrendous evil consequences given that he can easily do so. We would certainly see ourselves as morally obligated to do just that if we only had the power. Accordingly, the same should hold true of God.

Still, it might be objected that if God did intervene to the degree to which I am claiming he would have to be intervening, we would no longer be living in a world governed by natural laws, and so no longer be able to discover such laws and put that knowledge to work in our lives.[20]

Clearly, there is no denying that a world where God intervened, as needed, to prevent significant and especially horrendous evil consequences of immoral actions would be a different world from the one we currently inhabit.[21] But such a world would still have regularities. They would just be somewhat different from the regularities that hold in our world. Think of the fictional city of Metropolis in which Superman/ Clark Kent was imagined to live. Surely regularities did hold in that imaginary city. They were just different from the regularities that hold in our world because of the "to be expected" interventions of Superman that occurred in Metropolis. So if all the world were like Metropolis, we would still discover natural laws. We would just learn that the operation of those laws was subject to moral constraints because of the additional regular interventions of superheroes or God. The same would be true in an ideally just and powerful political state, where all murders, serious assaults, and so on would be prevented. There too natural law regularities governing human behavior would be constrained, so to speak, by the to-be-expected regular moral interventions of such a state. Of course, soul-making would still exist in Metropolis or in an ideally just and powerful state, as it does in our world. It is just that the opportunities for soul-making that would exist there would be limited to just those opportunities that morally good people would prefer to have. But clearly no one should be objecting to living under those regularities.

VIII

Now Alvin Plantinga's work on the logical problem of evil can usefully be re-interpreted as attempting to showing that God and the existence of some evil is logically compatible with the following moral principle:

Noninterference (NI)
Every moral agent has reason not to interfere with the free actions of wrongdoers when permitting the slightly harmful consequences of those actions would lead to securing some significant moral good, in some cases, maybe just that of the freedom of the wrongdoers themselves, or to preventing some significant moral evil.[22]

This moral principle which holds of ourselves should apply to God as well, thus permitting God not to interfere with our free actions when only their slightly evil consequences would lead to significant goods or to the prevention of significant evils, as, for example, when God's noninterference with a person's insult delivered in anger is subsequently followed with regret by the person and forgiveness by her victim or by someone else upbraiding the wrongdoer thereby dissuading him from more serious wrongdoing. This shows how the existence of God is clearly compatible with the existence of some moral evil when that moral evil that we seeking to reconcile with God's existence is the "slightly harmful consequences of the actions of wrongdoers." Yet, as we have seen, when the evil is not the slightly harmful consequences of the actions of wrong- doers but rather the significant, and especially the horrendous, conse- quences of such wrongdoing, as it may well be, NI will not serve to justify noninterference with the free actions of wrongdoers. In order for such noninterference to be justified, or possibly justified, in such cases, more needs to be established, or possibly established, about a greater evil that would be prevented or a greater good that would be achieved by permit- ting the evil consequences in such cases. We need a much stronger justi- fication, or possible justification, in terms of the prevention of a greater evil or the provision of a greater good to hold in order for the permission of evil to be justified, or possibly justified, in such cases. And this Plantinga does not provide.

Here, however, we sought to determine not whether God's existence is compatible with some significant and especially horrendous consequences of moral evil but rather whether God's existence is compatible with the distribution and amount of moral evil that exists in the world. That clearly is the more important and the more inclusive question. This led us to consider additional moral principles and considerations that apply to God and ourselves. Here are the main ones roughly in the order that were introduced in the chapter:

1. If God does not constrain the significant consequences of the actions of wrongdoers, and, as a result, the victims of such wrongdoing are deprived of the significant freedom they require for soul-making in this life, there is a need to provide them with a second-inning afterlife where they will have the significant freedom needed for soul-making.
2. It would be morally inappropriate to receive a heavenly afterlife, even after having suffered significant evils that were unchosen and unac- cepted, without first having gone through a soul-making where one

did what one could be reasonably expected to do to make oneself less unworthy of such a heavenly afterlife.

3. The moral goal is not to have unconstrained freedom but rather to have morally constrained freedom.
4. God and a just political state ought to prevent significant evil consequences whenever possible while allowing lesser evil consequences whose general prevention would interfere with people's significant freedom to be used by individuals for soul-making as far as possible.
5. The Pauline Principle's requirement never to do evil that good may come of it, understood to have its greatest moral force when it prohibits the doing or permitting of significant evil consequences, applies more unconditionally to God than to ourselves.

Now while the Pauline Principle does occupy center stage in the argument of this chapter, the other moral considerations that apply analogously to God and ourselves are still important. These considerations, by imposing additional moral requirements on God and ourselves, make it impossible to justify the widespread exceptions to the Pauline Principle that would be required in order to reconcile God with the moral evil in the world. Specifically, by requiring God to provide an opportunity for soul-making in a second-inning afterlife to those who were deprived of that opportunity in this life and by requiring everyone to find it morally inappropriate to enter the heavenly afterlife without first having and then taken advantage of the opportunities for soul-making, these moral requirements help us to better see the conflict that emerges when the Pauline Principle is applied to God.[23] It is under these constraints that the Pauline Principle, supported by the analogy of a just political state, shows that it would be impermissible for God to permit the significantly evil consequences of our immoral actions either as a means to prevent a greater evil (given that God could prevent the greater evil without permitting the lesser evil) or as a means to securing a good to which we are not entitled (given that we humans are always prohibited from doing just that).[24] Hence, there is a logical contradiction between the existence of God, our moral requirements, and what would have to be God's widespread failure to prevent the loss of significant freedoms in our world resulting from immoral actions.

Notes

1. "Ethical" and "moral" are used synonymously here.
2. Again, I am understanding significant freedoms to be primarily those freedoms a just political state would want to protect since that would fairly secure each person's fundamental interests.
3. Mark Murphy maintains that God could foresee evil without intending it. But that is not logically possible. If there is a God, everything that happens in the world is due to either God's active or his permissive will. So evil must occur because of God's permissible will. Furthermore, when God permits evil that he could otherwise prevent, he must be acting intentionally with respect to that evil. For us, after we have turned the trolley from the track where it would kill five to the track where it will just kill one, we (causally) cannot prevent the death of the one child that we foresee. But God in similar circumstances would always be able to causally prevent the death of both the five children and the one child. God is never stuck with just foreseeing the (external) consequences of any evil that he could not have intentionally acted to prevent. So it would be logically impossible for Murphy's perfect Anselmian God to foresee significant or especially horrendous evil consequences without intending them by permitting them. See Murphy (2016, p. 183).
4. Suppose we allow, as some Open theists do, that an all good, all powerful God may not be able to completely foresee the future (Hasker 2004). Still, when an external act with its morally evil consequences is coming into existence, God must be permitting that external act with its consequences. This implies God must intend not to prevent it, which further implies he is not merely foreseeing that act with its consequences.
5. See Swinburne (1998) and Lewis (2000).
6. This would still permit a great deal of moral evil in the world, primarily the moral evil of bad intentions. But neither God nor the state political state would be concerned to prevent this moral evil since it does not involve the afflicting of significant or especially horrendous evil consequences on the victims of wrongdoing.
7. See the Department of Homeland Security's March 2, 2016 report: https://www.dhs.gov/publication/future-attribute-screening-technology# (accessed 10/6/2018).
8. If someone were to object that there is no in-principle way of distinguishing between preventing evil and providing a good but that it is

always a matter of what description one employs, as two commentators, Frances Howard-Snyder and Stephen Wykstra, appropriately did with respect to an earlier version of this chapter, the next chapter shows how the two can be distinguished in principle.

9. There are a lot of trivial exceptions to the Pauline Principle like stepping on someone's foot to get out of a crowded subway to achieve some greater good.

10. An even more conclusive argument will be given for this conclusion in subsequent chapters.

11. See previous note.

12. The opportunity to engage in the virtuous behavior needed to make them less unworthy of a heavenly afterlife is however, at least in part, a gift to which we are not entitled. See Chap. 7 for further discussion.

13. This, of course, holds for those who are capable, given the opportunity, of doing what we could be reasonably expected to do to make themselves less unworthy of such a life through soul-making. For those who lack such a capacity something else may be morally appropriate.

14. Notice that if God had, in fact, met the requirement to prevent the loss of significant freedom, no one would have been deprived of the freedom necessary for soul-making in this life by the immoral actions of others, and so no one, on this account, would have been in need of a second-inning afterlife.

15. Of course, there are cases, such as that of Maya Angelou, where a person overcomes the effects of the significant moral evil inflicted upon them. Yet even in such cases, victims surely should have wished for a life where the evil consequences inflicted on them were prevented. This is because, among other things, they would need to take into account the effects on the wrongdoers themselves and how much better it would be for them, particularly if they later come to repent their actions, if God had prevented significant and especially horrendous evil consequences of their actions from being inflicted on their victims.

16. Interestingly, Thomas Aquinas endorses a similar limited role for a political state, maintaining that human law should not attempt to prevent "all evil," but "only the more grievous vices." See Aquinas (1947, Pt. I-II Q.96 Art 2).

17. As we noted earlier, these failings to prevent evil need not be understood to be exceptions to the Pauline Principle, but that does not affect their justification.

18. Strong as this argument is that God would not be morally justified in permitting the significant consequences of wrongful acts to attain a greater good; an even stronger argument will be given for this conclusion in the next two chapters which relies on a jointly exhaustive classification of all the possible goods at issue here.
19. For example, see Maitsen (2017, pp. 141–154).
20. For this objection, see Hick (1973, pp. 40–43) and Swinburne (1998, Chapter 10).
21. The "as needed" clause is there to indicate that whether God acts in this regard and the degree to which he does act depends on what we do.
22. Again, it should be noted that the freedoms of wrongdoers are not always significant moral goods. Sometimes the freedoms of wrongdoers are freedoms they should not have, and clearly in such cases, these freedoms are definitely not significant moral goods.
23. Useful though these additional premises are here, as we shall see, it is possible to support my logical argument against the existence of God primarily on minimal components of the Pauline Principle and the analogy of ideally just and powerful state, along with some more general premises.
24. Now it might be objected that this prohibition does not hold with respect to goods that can be provided to us only by God. In the next chapter, I will address this objection by considering what obtains with respect to such goods.

Bibliography

Aquinas, Thomas 1947. *Summa Theologiae*. Trans. The Fathers of the English Dominican Province. New York: Benziger Brother Inc.
Hasker, W. 2004. *Providence, Evil, and the Openness of God*. London: Routledge.
Hick, John. 1973. *Philosophy of Religion. Second Edition*. Englewood Cliffs: Prentice-Hall.
Lewis, David. 2000. Evil for Freedom's Sake. In *Papers in Ethics and Social Philosophy*, ed. Lewis. Cambridge, UK: Cambridge University Press.
Maitsen, Stephen. 2017. Perfection, Evil, and Morality. In *Ethics and the Problem of Evil*, ed. Sterba, 141–154. Bloomington: Indiana University Press.
Murphy, Mark. 2016. *God's Ethics*. New York: Oxford University Press.
Murray, M. 2008. *Nature Red in Tooth and Claw*. Oxford: Oxford University Press.
Swinburne, R. 1998. *Providence and the Problem of Evil*. Oxford: Clarendon Press.

5

Skeptical Theism to the Rescue?

Skeptical theists are theists who are skeptical about whether we could know the reasons God would have for permitting evil. The term "skeptical theism" was coined by Paul Draper, who is not a theist, but the term has come to be embraced by many philosophers who are theists.[1] Contemporary defenders include Alvin Plantinga, Stephen Wykstra, Peter van Inwagen, Michael Bergmann, and Daniel Howard-Snyder.[2] Since Michael Bergmann has developed a more structured account of the view, I will focus on his work.[3] However, what I have to say can be easily interpreted to apply to other formulations of skeptical theism as well.[4]

I

According to Bergmann, while some actions are morally wrong in themselves, there is a wide range of actions whose moral rightness or moral wrongness is determined simply by their overall consequences. So for the purposes of his defense of theism, Bergmann wants to focus on just those actions, setting aside consideration of actions that are morally wrong in themselves.[5] With respect to the actions that are purportedly morally

© The Author(s) 2019
J. P. Sterba, *Is a Good God Logically Possible?*,
https://doi.org/10.1007/978-3-030-05469-4_5

right or wrong simply in virtue of their overall consequences, Bergmann wants to apply the following skeptical theses:

ST1) We have no good reason for thinking that the possible goods we know of are representative of the possible goods there are.

ST2) We have no good reason for thinking that the possible evils we know of are representative of the possible evils there are.

ST3) We have no good reason for thinking that the entailment relations we know of between possible goods and the permission of possible evils are representative of the entailment relations there are between possible goods and the permission of possible evils.[6]

ST4) We have no good reason for thinking that the total moral value or disvalue we perceive in certain complex states of affairs accurately reflects the total moral value or disvalue they really have.[7]

Using these theses, Bergmann thinks he can undercut arguments from evil directed against theism that have the following form:

1. There are some evils that are such that humans can't think of any God-justifying reason for permitting them.
2. So probably there isn't any God-justifying reason for permitting those evils.
3. If God existed, he wouldn't permit those evils if there were no God-justifying reason for permitting them.
4. Therefore, probably God does not exist.[8]

To illustrate how Bergmann thinks his critique works, consider the following example. In Dostoyevsky's *Brothers Karamazov*, Ivan Karamazov tells of a child of eight living under Russian serfdom who throws a stone in play and causes the favorite hunting dog of his master, a retired General, to go lame (Dostoyevsky 1966, p. 219–220). The General then has the boy locked up overnight. The next morning the boy is brought out before all the General's servants, who are summoned for their edification, with his mother standing in front. The General then has the boy stripped naked and orders him to run. As the boy runs, the General sets his whole pack of dogs on him. They tear him to pieces right before his mother's eyes. Just picture that for a moment.

Clearly we can't think of any God-justifying reason for permitting the General's action either to prevent a greater evil or to achieve a greater good.[9] So the example does support (1). But can we then infer (2) from (1)? (2) maintains that the goods and evils we know of with respect to this case are, in fact, representative of the goods and evils there are. If we could make this inference from (1) to (2), we could easily move through (3) to (4) which is the conclusion of this argument against the existence of God.

However, Bergmann thinks that we cannot justify an inference from (1) to (2). He thinks that with respect to God-justifying reasons, ST1–3 blocks any move from a claim about the goods and evils we know of to a claim that our knowledge is representative of all the goods and evils there are. According to Bergmann, this is because God's knowledge of the consequences of permitting the General's action would so far outstrip our own that we could never make the claim that our knowledge is representative of God's knowledge in this regard.[10] Accordingly, by focusing on actions that he takes to be morally right or wrong simply in terms of their overall consequences, Bergmann thinks he can defeat the above argument against the existence of God that has long troubled theists.[11]

II

Yet even when consequences alone are being considered, as in Bergmann's argument, there is still the need to justify to the victims what would have to be God's permission of the infliction on them of at least the significant and especially the horrendous evil consequences of the actions of wrongdoers.[12] This arises from the very nature of morality which only justifies impositions that are reasonably acceptable to all those affected.[13]

Accordingly, one possible way that the infliction of harmful consequences on us might be justified is if we were to give our informed consent to them. This justification is used quite often in medical contexts.[14] Thus, patients give their informed consent to procedures that do impose pain and risk of harm on themselves in order to secure an expected compensating benefit. In addition, when patients cannot themselves give informed consent because they are underage or temporarily or permanently incompetent as adults then bona fide legal guardians are able to give the required informed consent for them in order to secure the expected compensating benefit.

However, when we consider what would have to be God's permission of the widespread infliction on victims of significant and especially horrendous evil consequences of immoral actions, nothing like informed consent typically obtains, at least not at the time God would be permitting the infliction of wrongful harm.[15] Of course, among Christians, Jesus is usually thought to have given his informed consent, or at least his willing acceptance, when suffering was imposed on him.[16] And so maybe those who suffer martyrdom, and at least some of those who suffer religious persecution, may be thought to be doing something similar.[17] Still, this clearly is a very small percentage of those on whom God would be permitting the infliction of significant and even horrendous evil consequences of immoral actions. How could this far greater number of cases be justified?

It would seem that these victims would have to be viewed to be incompetent throughout their entire earthly lives with respect to giving informed consent to significant and especially horrendous evil consequences that God would be permitting them to wrongfully suffer. Even so, if God's permission of the infliction of such evil consequences is to be justified then at some point these victims of wrongdoing need to be able to give their informed consent to what was done to them. Hence, even if we were to focus on actions that are purportedly justified simply in terms of their overall consequences, as Bergmann would have us do, there would still be the need to meet this requirement of informed consent, which for the overwhelming number of victims would have to be met only in the next life.[18]

Nor would it do to claim that God could have moral reasons for permitting significant and especially horrendous evil consequences of immoral actions to be inflicted on us that would be forever inaccessible to us. This is because reasons that would be forever inaccessible to us would not be moral reasons for permitting such consequences. Morality, as we noted earlier, only justifies impositions that are reasonably acceptable to *all* those affected. So moral reasons could only justify permitting such consequences if those permissions could be further shown, at some point, to be reasonably acceptable to *all* those affected. Only then could God's permission of significant and especially horrendous evil consequences of immoral actions be considered to be morally justified.

Here I am focusing on whether there would be a justification for God's not preventing, hence permitting, the final stage of significant and especially horrendous evil actions of wrongdoers, the stage where the wrongdoers would be imposing their evil consequences on their victims.[19] I am assuming that there would be a justification, at least in terms of freedom, for God's not interfering with the imaginings, intending, and even the taking of initial steps by wrongdoers toward bringing about significant and even horrendous evil consequences on their would-be victims. I am also assuming that there would be a justification, at least in terms of freedom, for God's not interfering when the consequences of immoral actions are not significantly evil.[20]

In addition, it turns out that actions that Bergmann wants us to focus on are far less relevant to a solution to the problem of evil than the actions that he sets aside. The actions that Bergmann sets aside are actions that are wrong in themselves and not simply because of any further bad consequences they might happen to have. As it turns out, it is the doing of such actions for the sake of further good consequences that is prohibited by the Pauline Principle's requirement never to do evil that good may come of it (Romans 3:8).[21] In fact, that God's permission of the infliction of the consequences of significantly evil actions seems to be prohibited by the Pauline Principle is even grounds for thinking that victims may never be able to give their informed consent to or find reasonably acceptable the infliction of such consequences on themselves.

Nor does understanding actions to be wrong in themselves require a specification of actions shorn of all consequences. Take a paradigm wrong-in-itself action of intentionally killing an innocent person. Such an action has the consequence that it is a killing that is both harmful and wrong built into it. So what the Pauline Principle prohibits is doing or permitting actions that simply have certain consequences built into them that are both harmful and wrong. These actions, so characterized, are already morally wrong and not just because of any further bad consequences that the actions might have. What the Pauline Principle prohibits is our ever doing such actions even for the sake of additional good consequences that the actions might have. Further, actions that are wrong in themselves violate their victim's rights and/or interests. Moreover, when there is no exception that permits doing an action that is wrong in itself, the rights that are violated by the action are significant and the interests violated are basic. It is for such actions, employing a more Kantian moral framework, we could say that the end does not justify the means.

Indeed, the few exceptions to the Pauline Principle that are allowed for us when significant moral evil is at stake are only allowed because we lack the power to avoid a greater moral evil by acting in any other way. For example, our inability to stop soldiers from torturing one child without exposing other children who are hiding nearby to being tortured themselves is crucial to justifying our inaction.[22] But clearly God would not be subject to any such limitation of power. God could prevent wrongful harm to all the children in this example. God does not have to choose between them. Consequently, none of the exceptions to the Pauline Principle that are permitted to agents, like ourselves, due to our limitations of power, would hold of God. This means that the Pauline Principle's prohibition of intentionally doing evil would be even more absolute in the case of God than it is for ourselves. Thus, the Pauline Principle, with its focus on prohibiting the doing or permitting of actions that are wrong in themselves, presents a significant challenge for a theistic solution to the problem of evil, one that is ignored by Bergmann with his focus on actions whose morality is purportedly dependent simply on their overall consequences.[23]

III

Without a doubt, a recurring objection to Bergmann's skeptical theism is that it leads to moral skepticism and thus undermines morality. Now it is easy to see why this objection has been so persistent. As we have noted, Bergmann wants us to focus on actions that purportedly are morally right or wrong simply in virtue of their overall consequences, setting aside consideration of actions that are morally wrong in themselves. Then after getting us to focus on just such actions, Bergmann informs us that we never really are in a good position to determine what are all the consequences of our actions, especially once we take into account that these consequences extend indefinitely into the future. That suggests the possibility that we never have the knowledge of consequences we need to determine what we morally ought to do, and that surely opens the door to moral skepticism. So to avoid moral skepticism, Bergmann needs to explain how we still know what we morally ought to do, given his consequences-focused view, when we have such limited access to many of the consequences of our actions.

Moreover, the persistent challenge of moral skepticism that Bergmann has had to face is to some extent of his own making. By setting aside actions that are wrong in themselves and focusing his attention on just those actions that he thinks are morally right or wrong simply in virtue of their overall consequences, Bergmann has deprived himself of just that part of morality that is most useful for meeting the challenge of moral skepticism. Actions that are wrong in themselves, unlike actions whose morality is highly dependent on their overall consequences, can provide a relatively quick and easily accessible verdict concerning what we ought to do. To his credit, Bergmann does recognize the usefulness of appealing to actions that are wrong in themselves.[24] Yet he uses this appeal sparingly, possibly recognizing that it presents a two-edged sword for his view. While such an appeal does help him deal with the problem of moral skepticism, it also suggests that actions that are wrong in themselves may have an important role to play with respect to the problem of evil, a role that Bergmann, however, never explores.

IV

Nevertheless, even when we recognize the need to deal with actions that are wrong in themselves, skeptical theism is not without resources. Here the crucial question is whether moral agents (God and ourselves, in particular) can permit significant moral evil to prevent a greater moral evil or to secure a greater moral good in violation of the Pauline Principle's requirement never to do evil that good may come of it.[25] Now virtually all of such exceptions to the Pauline Principle, as they apply to us, are understood to be of the first sort. They are cases where our justification for permitting a significant and even a horrendous moral evil is to prevent an even greater moral evil. This is because sometimes we are in a predicament where we can either causally prevent one significant or even horrendous evil or prevent another. Thus, consider the example I gave earlier where the only way we could stop soldiers from torturing one child would expose other children to torture who are hiding nearby. We could either rescue the one child from being tortured or we could prevent the other children from being tortured. Here, due to our limited causal powers, we would be led to permit the lesser moral evil in order to prevent the far greater moral evil. In comparable situations, however, God would always be able to prevent both moral evils. In the case we are considering, God could, for instance, arrange to have the soldiers spotted by opposing forces and then come under attack, and in this way enable all the children to get away safely.

Even so, there are some moral evils that logically could only exist if they were preceded by other moral evils. Thus, even God could not logically prevent a person from being brutally assaulted a second time without having permitted the person's being brutally assaulted a first time. Yet obviously this logical constraint does not, in itself, justify God's or anyone else's permitting the first brutal assault. In fact, if God prevented the first assault, the second one would never exist even in its initial stages to have its consequences prevented.[26] Moreover, as we have noted, God, unlike ourselves, is never justified in permitting significant and even horrendous evil consequences of one immoral action so as to prevent the greater evil consequences of another immoral action. This is because God could always prevent the significantly evil consequences of any immoral action that is being performed without permitting the significantly evil consequences of any other immoral action that would also be performed. God could do this by simply restricting people's freedom just enough to prevent the significant evil consequences of both actions. Accordingly, this, I claim, is just what God morally ought to do.

Now it might be objected that, for all we know, it could be just logically impossible for God to prevent the evil consequences of both immoral actions in such situations. This seems like something Bergmann might want to say, appealing to ST-3. Here the possible good in each case would be the prevention of the significant and especially the horrendous evil consequences of immoral actions. So the question is: Could there be entailment relations between such goods and permitting the consequences of other evils that would render it logically impossible for God to prevent both evil consequences? Yet notice how strange such entailment relations would be. Here we are dealing with situations where we lack the causal power to prevent the evil consequences of both immoral actions, and we appeal to that lack of causal power to justify why we permit the lesser evil consequence to prevent the greater evil consequence. Now, for just such situations, we are imagining that it is logically impossible for God to prevent the consequences of both immoral actions that are just causally impossible for us to prevent. Right off, that would make God impossibly less powerful than ourselves. Thus, we could imagine that we were to acquire new causal powers through technology to prevent both evil consequences in such contexts while God would be still stuck in a logical impossibility.[27]

If that isn't contradictory enough, suppose that it were logically impossible for God to prevent the evil consequences of both immoral actions A and B in situations where we cannot causally prevent both consequences. Then assuming that God did prevent the consequences of immoral action A would imply that action B with its consequences would be logically necessitated.[28] But for both compatibilists and incompatibilists, if an action is logically necessitated then it is not a free action, maybe not even an action at all.[29] So it turns out that assuming that it is logically impossible for God to prevent the evil consequences of both actions A and B leads to a contradiction: it implies that God could prevent the consequences of (free) action A and permit the consequences of (free) action B when, in fact, assuming that God did prevent the consequences of (free) action A, there logically could not be a (free) action B to have its consequences permitted. Hence, the skeptical theist assumption leads to two contradictory conclusions: one being that an all-powerful God is less powerful than we are, the other being that in contexts where we causally cannot prevent the evil consequences of both immoral actions, God could, and assuming that he did prevent the evil consequences of one of them, logically could not, permit the evil consequences of the other.[30]

So the assumption must be rejected. It must then be the case that God can always prevent the evil consequences of both actions in contexts where we, due to our limited causal power, can only prevent the evil consequences of one of them.[31] Hence, I have argued, it would be morally required for God to do so.[32]

Still, it might be objected that for any possible significant and especially horrendous consequences of immoral action that God might prevent—our example of soldiers' torturing children—that prevention might logically involve permitting a greater morally evil consequence that we don't know about. However, with regard to any such greater morally evil consequence, there would always be some creature or other, in the default case, the victim herself, who could have had the causal power to prevent that consequence.[33] Thus, human failure to prevent such evil consequences of immoral action is always due to lack of causal power.[34]

Even if we were facing the choice of preventing either the significant consequences of immoral action from being inflicted on some innocents or that of preventing the greater consequences of natural evil from being inflicted on other innocents, our inability to prevent both evils would still be causal or technological.

So what would explain God's failure to prevent such consequences? It couldn't be that God, like us, lacked the causal power to do so. Nor could it be that God is logically constrained from doing so when we are at best only causally constrained from doing so. This is because that would make God impossibly less powerful than we are. So God, if he existed, would have prevented such consequences. Yet clearly this has not happened.[35]

Thus, it looks like the only approach remaining to justifying God's permission of significant and especially horrendous evil is as a means to attaining some good rather than as a means to the prevention of some evil.[36] This may help explain why in the Bible the justification that is usually offered as to why God permits evil is not to prevent a greater moral evil, but rather to secure some moral good. Now it is important to see that the good here would have to be a good to which we are not entitled. This is because providing us with a good to which we are entitled is a way of not violating our rights which is also a way of preventing evil.[37] So we only get a real contrast between preventing an evil and providing a good when the good provided is not something to which we have a right.

V

Consider the story of Joseph, the son of Jacob, to which the final quarter of *The Book of Genesis* is devoted. Jacob shows favoritism for Joseph and that together with Joseph's recounting of dreams suggesting that his brothers would come to recognize him as having authority over them causes his brothers to hate him. So when Jacob sends Joseph on a mission to his brothers, they seize the opportunity and throw Joseph into a cistern intending to kill him. Later, when a caravan of traders heading to Egypt happens by, they decide to sell Joseph into slavery instead (Genesis, 37:1 to 50:26).

Now God surely could have prevented Joseph's brothers from wronging him in this way. For example, God could have arranged that the traders knew Jacob and his sons so that when the traders recognized what Joseph's brothers were planning to do to him, they could have freed Joseph from the cistern and returned him to his father. Instead, God permits Joseph to be wronged by his brothers by selling him into slavery.

Nevertheless, Joseph does manage to fare surprisingly well in Egypt and eventually through his ability to interpret dreams, particularly those of the Pharaoh, he is made the chief administrator over the land of Egypt. It is in this capacity that Joseph next encounters his brothers who have journeyed to Egypt to buy much needed grain. But while Joseph recognizes his brothers, they do not recognize him. So after testing them and discerning a change of heart concerning what they had done to him, Joseph reveals himself to them. He is then able to bring his entire extended family to Egypt where they can live under his protection.

The Bible clearly presents the story of Joseph as a justified case of God's permitting evil that good may come of it. Consider that the wrong done to Joseph enables him to use his unique abilities to advance himself in Egypt and later to provide for all the sons of Jacob from which the twelve tribes of Israel are said to descend. This is surely considerably more than Joseph would have been likely to accomplish if he had just lived out his pastoral life in Canaan.[38] Still, it is arguable that God could have saved the sons of Jacob and given them and their descendants their special mission without permitting Joseph to be sold into slavery. Thus, suppose when the sons of Jacob journeyed to Egypt to buy grain during the years of famine that Joseph (who had somehow been protected by God and not sold into slavery) was with them. Suppose, while in Egypt, Joseph, through his ability to interpret dreams, impresses whomever was the chief administrator in Egypt, and that administrator then provides protection to Joseph's entire extended family as in the biblical story. We would then get much the same good results as in the biblical story without the evil means.

Accordingly, it is hard to see how the story of Joseph helps us to account for what would have to be God's permission of the seemingly countless number of significant and especially horrendous evil consequences of immoral actions, which we have witnessed throughout the course of human history, right up to the present day. Here the reality is that the significantly morally evil consequences that God would have to be permitting to be inflicted on victims are frequently debilitating and dehumanizing, unlike in the case of Joseph, and that the goods that would serve to justify God's permission of these evil consequences are almost never triumphantly displayed, as in the case of Joseph.[39] It also bears noting here that in human contexts, justified cases of doing or permitting evil that an additional good may come of it all seem to be cases where the evil is not significant. So the possibility of finding a way that God could be morally justified in permitting significant and especially horrendous morally evil consequences to bring about some additional moral good does not look very promising at all.

VI

Even so, let us approach the question a bit differently. Let us ask what sort of moral good could conceivably justify God's permission of significant and especially horrendous evil consequences of immoral actions? Here, at least initially, there seems to be no limit to what moral goods might be in play in such contexts, and this is surely the way that Bergmann sees it. Nevertheless, upon reflection, it turns out that we really do have much more knowledge here than we might initially have thought.[40]

Clearly, according to Christian orthodoxy, the greatest moral good of all would be God's providing us with the heavenly afterlife itself with its option for divine friendship.[41] Surely nothing could be better for us than that. Even so, it would only be morally appropriate for us to enter a heavenly afterlife after we have done what we could be reasonably expected to do to make ourselves less unworthy of such a life through soul-making.[42] This soul-making would require, among other things, that we do what we can to achieve and maintain morally good and just relations with our fellow human beings. Since we cannot be forced to do this (such relations must be voluntarily chosen), God cannot guarantee that we will receive the heavenly afterlife.[43] At most, what God can guarantee is that we all have an adequate opportunity for soul-making so that we could do what we could be reasonably expected to do to make ourselves less unworthy of a heavenly afterlife. Accordingly, it would not be morally appropriate for us to receive a heavenly afterlife simply for unwillingly suffering the consequences of significant and especially horrendous evil actions.[44] Hence, the greatest moral good that God could appropriately provide us with is an opportunity for soul-making which we could then use to do what we could be reasonably expected to do to make ourselves less unworthy of a heavenly afterlife.

Now the question is: Could the provision of an opportunity for soul-making depend on God's permitting wrongdoers to inflict significant and especially horrendous evil consequences on their victims? Clearly, some opportunities for soul-making do logically depend on others having committed significant and even horrendous evils. For example, one cannot console a rape victim unless someone has raped the person one is consoling. Nor could one forgive a hate crime if no one actually committed such a crime. Yet this does not show that the provision of an opportunity for the soul-making requiring us to do what we could be reasonably expected to do to make ourselves less unworthy of a heavenly afterlife should depend on God's permitting wrongdoers to inflict significant or even horrendous evil consequences on their victims.

Here it would be useful to distinguish two different forms that an opportunity for soul-making can take. Let us call the first the "natural opportunity for soul-making." This is the opportunity each of us must have in order to become a good and just human being. It secures for each of us the opportunity to live a decent life ourselves and also to contribute to others doing the same as far as we could be reasonably expected to do so. This natural opportunity for soul-making is something to which we have a right, a right that can be pressed against our fellow human beings who happen to have more resources than they themselves need for a decent life.[45] Now the provision of this good is a way of not violating people's rights, which is also a way of not doing moral evil. So its nonprovision by someone who alone could provide it without denying anyone's rights would itself be morally evil.[46] However, what we are looking for here is a good the nonprovision of which would not be morally evil. Fortunately, a second form of the opportunity for soul-making is just such a good.

Let us call this second form a "Godly opportunity for soul-making." It is not an opportunity that we are entitled to receive. So its nonprovision would not be morally evil. It can only come by way of the grace of God. It is a gift that opens up to us the possibility of a personal relationship with the deity.

Could then our receiving this good be conditional on God's permitting significant and especially horrendous evil consequences of immoral actions? Must we ourselves, or others, commit significant and especially horrendous immoral actions whose evil consequences God permits before God could then provide us with a Godly opportunity for soul-making?

First, it would be morally inappropriate for our receiving a Godly opportunity for soul-making to be conditional on God's permitting significant and especially horrendous evil consequences of immoral actions. This is because it would give us the incentive to commit, and want others to commit, significant and even horrendous evil actions, virtually without limit, so that God would permit their consequences and thereby make possible our receiving a Godly opportunity for soul-making.[47] It would also support perverse incentives for God as well. Assuming that God wanted to provide us with a Godly opportunity for soul-making, God would also have to perversely want us to commit significant and even horrendous morally evil actions, virtually without limit, so that God could then permit their consequences and thereby make possible our receiving a Godly opportunity for soul-making.[48]

This arrangement would also be counterproductive, even contradictory. It would be counterproductive because the very means by which we would receive a Godly opportunity for soul-making, which is our commission of significant and even horrendous morally evil actions and God's permission of their consequences, would itself render us less unworthy of receiving a Godly opportunity for soul-making. It would be contradictory because making ourselves less unworthy of receiving a Godly opportunity for soul-making requires us to wish we had never done evil but we can't do that if we know that our doing evil and God's permitting it is a necessary means for God's providing us with a Godly opportunity for soul-making.

Second, given that a Godly opportunity for soul-making is something to which we are not entitled, something to which we do not have a right, its provision cannot be conditional on the violation of anyone's rights.[49] This is because even the provision of something to which we do have a right cannot be conditional on the violation of anyone's rights.[50] Take, for example, the provision of the right to liberty to which we all have a right.[51] The provision of that right cannot be conditional on the violation of anyone's rights.[52] All the more so, then, for the provision of something to which we do not have a right, like a Godly opportunity for soul-making. It clearly cannot be conditional on doing or permitting the violation of anyone's rights. Accordingly, the provision of a Godly opportunity for soul-making cannot be conditional on the violation of people's rights that would result from God's permission of significant and especially horrendous evil consequences of immoral actions.

Now it might be objected here that, for all we know, it could just be logically impossible for God to both provide us with a Godly opportunity for soul-making, something to which we do not have a right and to prevent horrendous evil consequences of immoral actions from being inflicted on us, something to which we do have a right.[53] Again, this seems to be something that Bergmann might want to say. Yet again notice how strange this claim would be. Clearly, it is difficult for us to even think of cases where we causally cannot provide others with goods to which they do not have a right unless we permit them to be deprived of goods to which they do have a right. Yet, it is for just such analogous cases that we are to imagine that God logically cannot provide us with something to which we do not have a right without permitting us to be deprived of something to which we do have a right. Again, that makes God look impossibly less powerful than ourselves. Thus, we could easily imagine that we never do suffer from this sort of causal inability (which may be not too far from the truth) while God would be still stuck in a logical impossibility in analogous contexts.

Again, if that isn't contradictory enough, suppose that this skeptical theist assumption was true, which implies that God could both prevent horrendous evil consequences of immoral actions from being inflicted on us while not providing us with a Godly opportunity for soul-making, But then assuming that God did prevent horrendous evil consequences of immoral actions from being inflicted on us, it would be logically necessitated that God not provide us with a Godly opportunity for soul-making. Yet, as we saw before, any action that is logically necessitated is not a free action, and maybe not even an action at all. This would mean that God would not be acting freely, or even acting at all, with respect to our having a Godly opportunity for soul-making. Hence, this skeptical theist assumption would lead to two contradictory conclusions: one being that God is less powerful than we are, the other being that in contexts where we normally can causally avoid violating the rights of others while providing them with something to which they do not have a right, God could, and assuming that he did prevent the horrendously evil consequences of our actions, logically could not choose to provide us with a Godly opportunity for soul-making, something to which we do not have a right.[54] So the assumption must be rejected.

Therefore, it must be the case that God can both provide us with a Godly opportunity for soul-making, something to which we do not have a right and prevent horrendous evil consequences of immoral actions from being inflicted on us, something to which we do have a right.[55] That being the case, there are no grounds at all for making the provision of a Godly opportunity for soul-making, something to which we do not have a right, conditional upon God's not preventing horrendous evil consequences of immoral actions from being inflicted on us, given that we have a right to that prevention by anyone who could do so. Put another way, the provision of a good that is supererogatory, or even beyond the supererogatory, like a Godly opportunity for soul-making, cannot be conditional on God's failing to provide something whose provision is obligatory.[56] Providing supererogatory or beyond goods cannot be legitimately secured by failing to provide goods that are obligatory, and thus should be provided.

Moreover, if we were to assume that it is logically impossible for God to prevent significant and especially horrendous evil consequences of immoral actions, then God could not be permitting those consequences either because God could only permit what he could also prevent. But that contradicts a fundamental doctrine of traditional theism that God permits moral evil.

Still, given that a Godly opportunity for soul-making is supposed to be a free gift, it really would have to be up to God who would receive it. Now we might think that if God provided this opportunity to any of us, fairness would require that it be provided to all of us. Certainly, among Christians, the currently prevailing view is that this opportunity is offered to all, but that would presumably imply that many would only receive that offer in an afterlife where soul-making continues to go on.[57]

Nevertheless, assuming that a Godly opportunity for soul-making is a free gift, something to which we do not have a right, it also must *not* be something that is absolutely required for our fundamental well-being. If it were something that is absolutely required for our fundamental well-being, then we would have a right to it analogous to the way we have a right to liberty or a right to welfare. God then, who alone could provide us with that opportunity, would be morally required to do so on relatively easy terms, as obtains in other cases where we do have a right to something. However, if a Godly opportunity for soul-making is really a free gift, and thus not something to which we have a right, we must then be able to have a decent life without it. This in turn means that we could have such a life without the special friendship with God that the appropriate use of that opportunity is supposed to make us less unworthy of. Presumably then, by just using well a natural opportunity for soul-making (to which we do have a right), we should be able to have a decent life both here and in any here-after. Thus, the fact that a Godly opportunity for soul-making is not something that is required for a decent life would constitute yet another reason why God's provision of that opportunity could not be conditional on his permitting wrongdoers to inflict significant and especially horrendously evil consequences of their actions on their victims. The provision of something to which we do not have a right, and so can live decently without, morally cannot be provided to us at the cost of something to which we do have a right and so we should not have to live without.

Summing up, then, what I have argued is that it would be morally inappropriate for God to just provide us with a heavenly afterlife irrespective of whether or not we did what we could be reasonably expected to do to make ourselves less unworthy of it. Accordingly, the greatest moral good that God could appropriately provide us with is a Godly opportunity for soul-making which we could then use to do what could be reasonably expected of us to make ourselves less unworthy of a heavenly afterlife. I further argued that it would be morally inappropriate if the provision of a Godly opportunity for soul-making were conditional on God's permitting significant and especially horrendous evil consequences of immoral actions. This is because it would give us an incentive to commit, and want others to commit, significant and especially horrendous evil actions virtually without any limit, and it would likewise support perverse incentives for God as well. I also argued that because a Godly opportunity for soul-making is not something to which we have a right, its provision cannot be conditional on the violation of anyone's rights. The same holds true, of course, for the provision of any other good to which we do not have a right. Hence, the provision of a Godly opportunity for soul-making or the provision of any other good to which we do not have a right could not justifiably depend on God's permission of the infliction of significant and especially horrendous evil consequences of immoral actions on their victims. Nevertheless, the most telling reason it would be morally inappropriate for God to make the provision of a Godly opportunity for soul-making, or any other good to which we do not have a right, conditional on God's permitting significant and especially horrendous evil consequences of immoral action is that there are countless morally unobjectionable ways that God could provide that same opportunity to us.[58]

So is there anything else we could add to this case for the logical incompatibility of our morality, the existence of God, and God's permission of significant and especially horrendous evil consequences of immoral actions throughout history, right up to the present moment? As it turns out, there is.

VII

Historically, the problem of evil has focused on what would be God's relationship to evil, especially what would be God's relationship to significant and especially horrendous evil consequences of immoral actions. That is clearly an appropriate focus. Surely, God should be concerned to prevent significant and especially horrendous evil consequences of immoral actions as much as possible. In turn, these reflections have given rise to the question: Why would God permit, rather than prevent, the significant and especially the horrendous evil consequences of immoral actions? Here, I have argued that there is no justification for God's permitting, rather than preventing, such moral evil in order to prevent a greater moral evil because God could always just prevent the consequences of both moral evils. I have also argued that there is no justification for God's permitting, rather than preventing, such moral evil for the sake of securing the moral good that I have called a Godly opportunity for soul-making to which we do not have a right and other such goods because there is a moral objection to the provision of such goods such means when morally unobjectionable means are available.

Yet there is a related question that is rarely asked: Beyond creation, why would God not do moral good, not just by way of permitting moral evil, but directly, just because it is the right thing to do. For example, consider what I have called a natural opportunity for soul-making. This is the opportunity each of us needs in order to become a good and just human being. The provision of this natural opportunity for soul-making is a moral good to which we have a right, a right that can be pressed against our fellow human beings who happen to have more resources than they themselves require for a decent life. But if a right to this moral good can be pressed against our fellow humans, why could it not be pressed against God as well? Unlike our fellow humans, God would seemingly never lack the resources to provide us with a natural opportunity for soul-making.[59] So why wouldn't God have an obligation to do so, an obligation that we can see, in an overwhelming number of cases, has been left unfulfilled?

VIII

Now it might be objected that if God were to directly provide us with a natural opportunity for soul-making that would eliminate any need for us to do so ourselves. Thus, suppose, using a different example from the one used in the last chapter, that you had done all that you could to provide someone with a natural opportunity for soul-making, including enough to eat and a place to stay and you could see that you were not going to be completely successful.[60] Suppose that God were then to intervene and provide the extra resources that are needed. Presumably, you would be happy with God's intervention in such a case.

Yet imagine you are later considering whether to intervene again to provide someone else with of a natural opportunity for soul-making. You might reason that if you did intervene you might well be successful this time. Yet upon further reflection, you might decide that there really is no need for you to do so because if you do nothing, you now assume that God would again intervene as he had done before and meet the need. So you do nothing.

According to some theists, this is just the sort of behavior we would expect if God were to regularly intervene to produce good consequences in such cases. Hence, they claim, this explains why God does not normally intervene to do good in this way. If God did intervene, on their account, we would lose the motivation we have to intervene ourselves, and thereby fail to utilize the opportunities we have for soul-making.

Now I maintain that rather than always intervening or always not intervening God should be engaging in what I would call constrained intervention. To see how this would work, consider again the second case where you decided not to intervene to do good yourself on the assumption that God would meet the need as he had, in part, done before when you were trying your best but were not going to be successful at providing what is needed on your own. Suppose what happens next is not exactly what you had expected. Yes, God does intervene to do good, but that intervention is only partly successful. Originally, let's say, on this second occasion, you were in a position to provide immediately for the deserving person's basic needs. Now that you have chosen to do nothing, you see, as you walk by, that the person's needs are still unmet. However, subsequently you learn that a wealthy person, somewhat inexplicably, just happens to show up some hours later and completely met all the person's basic needs. So you assume, not unreasonably, that God was involved in this intervention as well as in the earlier one. Nevertheless, you cannot help but note that this second intervention was not as completely successful as it presumably would have been if you had chosen to intervene yourself. After all, you could have helped the person immediately. As a result, the poor person would not have suffered during the intervening hours before being helped.

So you begin to detect a pattern. When you choose to intervene to do good yourself, either you will be completely successful or your intervention will fall short. When the latter is going to happen, God does something to make the intervention completely successful.[61] Likewise, when you choose not to intervene to provide deserving people what they need when you could do so, God again intervenes but this time not in a fully successful way. In cases of this sort, there is a residue of bad consequences that the victim still does suffer. This residue is not a significant rights violation itself, but it is harmful nonetheless, and it is something for which you are primarily responsible. In our example, you could have provided the needed goods earlier, but you chose not to do so, and that makes you responsible for the consequences. Of course, God too could have provided the needed goods earlier when you decided not to provide them yourself. It is just that in such cases, God has chosen not to fully intervene and completely provide what is needed in order to leave you with an opportunity for soul-making. Moreover, I maintain that this is exactly what God would be required to do here: Provide us with the natural opportunities for soul-making to which we have a right, as needed, while, at the same time, not making the provision of other opportunities for soul-making to which we do not have a right (e.g., the Godly opportunities) conditional upon God's permission of significant and especially horrendous consequences of immoral actions.[62]

IX

Now it might be objected that we have a moral obligation to turn to God and that when we don't do so, God is morally justified in permitting the infliction of significant or horrendous evil consequences of immoral action on us to get us to abide by that obligation.[63] However, moral obligations can only be established against a background of morally appropriate, generally benevolent and protective behavior. Absent that behavior by any assumed deity, as evidenced by what would have to be the widespread violations of exceptionless minimal components of the Pauline Principle, then no such background condition obtains. Moreover, even if we were justified in believing that God created us, that would not be enough, all by itself, to ground such an obligation. Being a protector and a benefactor is also required. Consider the analogy of parents who simply procreate children but then fail to care for them or protect them when they could easily do so. Surely we would not think that their children, if somehow they managed to survive, would be under a moral obligation to seek out their biological parents and become friends with them. The same would hold for any mere creator God, who, then of course, could not be the all-good, all-powerful God of traditional theism.[64]

X

So in the end, how might Bergmann respond to the above argument? He might say (because he has said this in another context) that skeptical theism is directed only at inductive inferences from God-justifying reasons we can think of to the conclusion that there are no God-justifying reasons for permitting significant and especially horrendous evil consequences of immoral actions (Bergmann 2014, p. 210). My argument, Bergmann might say, has the form of a logical argument against the existence of God.[65] It appeals to requirements of morality and shows how these requirements are incompatible with an all-good, all-powerful God. Yet clearly such a response by Bergmann would be beside the point.[66] If there is a successful deductive argument against the existence of God, who would care about a skeptical critique of an inductive argument from evil, especially when that critique is based on an inaccurate assessment of the moral requirements at issue?[67]

Fortunately, it is possible to piece together a more direct response to the argument of this chapter from Bergmann's work. First, Bergmann does defend certain constraints on pursuing overall good consequences. For example, when responding to the objection that his skeptical theism puts no limit on how much evil God might permit in the world, Bergmann counters that God would not permit suffering, or presumably any significant and especially any horrendous evil consequences of immoral actions, "unless the sufferer's life is on the whole good" (Bergmann 2009, p. 391). This is a constraint on God's permission of significant and especially horrendous evil consequences of immoral acts that is not grounded in overall good consequences. Yet, by itself, it is inadequate. For example, God's just providing Rachel with a heavenly afterlife after Rachel has done what she could be reasonably expected to do to make herself less unworthy of a heavenly afterlife would not be enough. It would also have to be case that God was not permitting Rachel to suffer unnecessarily from significant and especially horrendous evil consequences of immoral actions of others. Our morality thus requires a stronger constraint against unnecessary suffering. What it requires is the constraint that I set out at the very beginning of this chapter, which is that morality only justifies impositions that are reasonably acceptable to all those affected. This constraint would rule out Rachel's being unnecessarily harmed, irrespective of whether or not after she had gone through a process of soul-making, God had provided her with a heavenly afterlife.[68]

Second, employing a parent-child analogy, Bergmann claims that it would be morally permissible for God in virtue of his special relationship to us as Creator to permit us to experience significant and even horrendous evil consequences of immoral actions when it would not be permissible for others to do the same for the sake of the overall good consequences that might result therefrom (Bergmann 2009, pp. 292–293). This is another constraint on permitting evil, but it too would have to be expanded further to include the more general constraint, just mentioned, such that those on whom God permits the infliction of significant and especially horrendous evil consequences of immoral actions should at some point find God's permission of those afflictions reasonably acceptable, and it would not be reasonably acceptable if God could have easily have prevented those consequences while still being able either to prevent a greater evil or to provide a greater good by morally unobjectionable means.

Third, Bergmann claims that God may have to permit significant and especially horrendous consequences of some evil actions in order to prevent a greater evil (Bergmann 2012, pp. 18–19). Bergmann even suggests that our inability to grant that this is the case may be due to a failure of imagination on our part. He says:

> Perhaps on some objective scale of badness the horrors of cancer treatment are at level 10 and the horrors of the long-term enslavement and raping of Sudanese girls and of the Nazi treatment of Jews in the Holocaust are between 85 and 100. And perhaps the ability of humans to take in such suffering and accurately assess its badness tops out when the horrors reach the 100 or 200 or 500 level. Perhaps being exposed to vivid portrayals of things that are objectively more horrifying than that causes us to be overwhelmed and to begin to shut down emotionally and cognitively. Even so, things would be otherwise with God. God, if he exists, would be able to take in and accurately evaluate horrors at a level of one million and beyond, horrors we can't imagine and are not capable, psychologically, of taking in. And if God were to permit some evil on the level of 100 or 500 because he knew that was the only way to prevent some evil on the level of one million, no morally decent person would object to that any more than they would object to a parent's choice to let her child undergo painful treatment for cancer. (Ibid., p. 22)

Here Bergmann is failing to take into account that God, as I have argued, would always be in a position with respect to moral evils to prevent significant and especially horrendous consequences of all such evils that are causally related. Unlike us, whose causal powers are limited, God could always prevent all the significant and especially the horrendous evil consequences of immoral actions; God would never have to permit such consequences of some immoral actions in order to prevent greater evil consequences of some other immoral actions. All God would have to do is restrict the external freedom of the agents in each case, something either you or I could do as well if we only had the power.[69]

Fourth, this just leaves open the possibility of God justifiably permitting significant and even horrendous evil consequences of immoral actions to achieve some moral good. I have argued that the moral good at stake here has to be one that can't be redescribed as the prevention of a moral evil. So it has to be a good to which we do not have a right, like the provision of a Godly opportunity for soul-making. Now Bergmann doesn't often talk about the possibility of God permitting moral evil to bring about some moral good that cannot be redescribed as the prevention of some moral evil. But when he can be so interpreted, he professes that we have "to own up to near complete ignorance as to what those goods could be."[70] By contrast, in this chapter, I have argued that Christian orthodoxy purports to give us considerable knowledge about what those goods are.[71] Thus, according to this orthodoxy, the greatest moral good of all that we could receive is the heavenly afterlife itself providing us with friendship with God. However, in this regard, I have argued that it would be morally inappropriate for us to receive this good of a heavenly afterlife just outright without having first done what we could be reasonably expected to do to make ourselves less unworthy of a such an afterlife through a process of soul-making. It follows that the greatest moral good that God can actually provide us with is a Godly opportunity of soul-making, an opportunity to which we do not have a right. I further argued that it would not be morally appropriate for God to make the provision of a Godly opportunity for soul-making to which we do not have a right dependent on his permitting significant and especially horrendous evil consequences of immoral actions, especially given that a Godly opportunity for soul-making could be provided to us in countless other ways that are morally unobjectionable. Unfortunately, Bergmann never considers this sort of argument.

Fifth, Bergmann has nothing to say about the positive obligations I have claimed God would have with respect to us. Like most contemporary philosophers of religion, Bergmann seems never to have considered the possibility that God's obligations to us might extend beyond simply preventing the infliction of significant and especially horrendous evil consequences on us to actually providing us with the good of a natural opportunity for soul-making, when needed, to which we have a right.[72]

The upshot is that Bergmann's attempt to rescue theism by undercutting a particular inductive argument from evil is of little use in the face of a successful deductive argument from evil, especially one that exposes the faulty moral foundation underlying Bergmann's own attempt.

XI

Let me conclude by returning to the example from Dostoyevsky's *Brothers Karamazov* that I used to illustrate Bergmann's skeptical theism at the beginning of this chapter. Applying the argument of the chapter to this example, I think we can now see that God's permission of the consequences of the General's horrendous immoral action could not be morally justified for the following reasons:

1. God's permission of the evil consequences of the General's action could not be a morally acceptable means to prevent some other greater evil consequences of an immoral action. This is because God, being all-powerful, could always prevent the evil consequences of any action, as needed, by just sufficiently restricting the external freedom of the evildoer in each case. Hence, this is just, I claim, what God morally should do.
2. Neither could God's permission of the morally evil consequences of the General's action be a morally justified means to secure some good to which we are not entitled. This is because the greatest good to which we are not entitled that God could morally provide us with would be a Godly opportunity for soul-making, and to make the provision of that good, and other such goods to which we do not have a right, conditional on God's permission of significant and especially horrendous evil consequences of immoral actions, like the General's, would lead to morally perverse incentives for us and for God as well. In addition, making the provision of a Godly opportunity for soul-making, and other such goods to which we do not have a right, conditional on the permission of significant and especially horrendous evil consequences of immoral actions, like the General's, would not be morally justified because we do not have a right to such goods, and so clearly their provision could not be conditional on the violation of anyone's

rights, especially when there are countless other ways that these goods could be provided that are not morally objectionable.

Hence, there is no way for God's permission of the horrendously evil consequences of the General's actions to be morally justified. In this way, we can explain the intuitive force that Dostoyevsky's example has had on so many of us by showing the logical incompatibility of morality with what would have to be a shocking instance of God's widespread permission of significant and especially horrendous evil consequences of immoral actions.

Notes

1. See Draper (1996, pp. 175–192). The basic idea can found in *Job*. There Job wants an explanation as to why God permitted so much evil to be inflicted on him. God responds by challenging Job as to how he could presume to be able to know God's reasons for acting:

> Who is this that darkens counsel
>   by words without
>   knowledge?
> Where were you when I laid the
>   foundations of the earth?
> Is it your wisdom that the
>   hawk soars,
>   and spreads its wings toward
>   the south?
> Is it at your command that the
>   eagle mounts up
>   and makes its nest on high?
>   (Job 38).

2. See Plantinga (1974), Wykstra (1984, pp. 73–84, 1996), Wykstra with Perrine (2012, pp. 375–399), van Inwagen (1988, pp. 161–187, 2006 pp. 278–296), Bergmann (2001, pp. 278–296, 2009, pp. 375–399), Howard-Snyder (2009, pp. 286–310).
3. See also Bergmann and Rea (2005, pp. 241–250), Bergmann (2012, 2014, pp. 209–220).

4. It makes sense to take up the skeptical theist challenge to the probabilistic argument from evil even though I am defending a logical argument from evil because the same skeptical strategy that the skeptical theist uses against the one argument could also be directed at the other. So I must meet the challenge.

5. See, in particular, Bergmann (2014, pp. 211–212, 214, 220).

6. As far as I can tell, there are two relevant senses of permitting evil here. According to the first, we can say X permits Y to do evil if X removes whatever legal and/or moral obstacle there is to Y's doing evil. In these cases, the evil can be a natural evil, as in the case of a parent giving her permission to have her child undergo a painful operation in an attempt to save the child's life. Here too it is possible for the evil not to obtain after permission for it has been given. Thus, in the case just given, the child may die before the operation can be performed. However, this sense is less relevant to the problem of evil. Unlike human authorities, God is not usually thought to be in the business of removing moral and legal obstacles to our doing of evil. However, according to the second sense of permitting evil, we can say X permits Y to do evil, for example, the immoral consequences of Y's wrongdoing, if X does not prevent those consequences from happening when X could otherwise do so. In this sense, if X permits Y to do evil, unlike the first sense, the evil that X permits definitely does happen. Now it is this second sense of permitting evil that, I claim, is most relevant to the problem of evil. This is because it is God's permission of evil in this sense, by not actually preventing, say, the evil consequences when he could otherwise do so, that can be morally problematic when those evil consequences are significantly and especially when they are horrendously evil. It is this second sense of permitting evil that I take it is employed in the first premise of this argument against the existence of God.

7. See, in particular, Bergmann (2009, pp. 376–379).

8. See, in particular, Ibid., p. 374.

9. What we can imagine is God's preventing the consequences of the General's evil action by, say, diverting the hounds from attacking the boy with the sudden appearance of a fox.

10. See, in particular, Bergmann (2009, pp. 375–381).

11. It is worth noting that Bergmann thinks that the same skeptical "bag of tricks" that he uses in his attempt to defeat the above probabilistic argument against the existence the existence of an all-good, all-powerful

deity, could also be used to defeat a comparable probabilistic argument against the existence of an all-evil, all-powerful deity. See his response to an earlier questioner at Plantinga's Retirement Conference 2010 http://philreligion.nd.edu/videos/conference-videos/alvin-plantinga-retirement-celebration/. Accessed 10/6/2018.

12. This is just the kind of justification that Marilyn Adams thinks must obtain if God's permission of such evils is to be morally defensible. See Adams (1999).

13. See Sterba (2005, Chapters 1–5).

14. See Faden and Beauchamp (1986), Buchanan and Brock (1989), O'Neill (2002).

15. Notice too that in standard informed consent cases, one is consenting to something that would not be morally wrong if one consents to it. However, nothing similar seems to obtain in the cases we are considering.

16. Luke tells us that Jesus prayed in the Garden of Gethsemane, contemplating what was to befall him: "Father, if you are willing, take this cup from me; yet not my will, but yours be done" (Luke 22:41–42). Matthew records Jesus praying: "My Father, if it is not possible for this cup to be taken away unless I drink it, may your will be done" (Matt. 26:42). Mark puts it differently "Abba, Father," he said, "everything is possible for you. Take this cup from me. Yet not what I will, but what you will" (Mark 14:36). All give evidence of Jesus's informed acceptance of what was soon to befall him.

17. There is also the worry that even in these cases, although there is consent, it is not sufficiently informed. That is a concern, but the absence of anything like consent in the far greater number of cases is even more significant.

18. The requirement of informed consent is only a necessary condition for moral justification. It may be met even when the more inclusive requirement of being an imposition that is reasonably acceptable to all those affected is not. Notice too that I start this section by affirming that morality requires reasonable acceptability to those affected, then allow that giving one's informed consent is a way of meeting this requirement under certain conditions, before concluding that giving informed consent at some time or other by those who are capable of doing so is just a necessary condition for meeting morality's reasonable acceptability requirement.

19. Now a number of years ago, Steven Boer argued that God could allow us our free choices and just prevent all the consequences of our immoral actions. When critics objected to Boer's proposal on grounds that it too severely limited our freedom, Robert McKim suggested that the criticism could be met by modifying Boer's proposal to having God just prevent the "dreadful" consequences of our immoral actions. This, of course, is similar to what I claiming God should do. But McKim then went on to allow that his own modification of Boer's proposal could itself be defeated by a theodicy that showed that it would be morally better for God to permit rather than to prevent even the dreadful consequences of our immoral actions. Now in this chapter, I show why no such theodicy is possible. See Boer (1978, pp. 110–112), Coughlan (1979, pp. 58–60), Dilley (1982, pp. 355–364), McKim (1984, pp. 164–170).

20. For my purposes, I am including the "outer manifestation of the act" sometimes referred to as the "external act" as either including or as part of the consequences of an act.

21. See also Finnis (1991).

22. Here we would be (intentionally) omitting to help the one child in order to save the others from a similar fate.

23. It is also arguable that there are no actions whose morality is simply dependent on their consequences. This would mean that all our actions are morally constrained by nonconsequential requirements and that it is only within those constraints that sometimes consequences can be taken into account to further determine what is morally required, permissible, or just ideal. For God, however, given the unlimited options available to him, such nonconsequential constraints can be met without sacrificing overall good consequences.

24. Bergmann in his joint article with Rea even appeals to divine command theory to meet the challenge of moral skepticism. Bergmann and Rea seem to recognize, however, that such an appeal undercuts their claim that the skeptical component of their argument for skeptical theism can be endorsed by theists and atheists alike. See Bergmann and Rea (2005 pp. 244–245).

25. It is worth noting that the course of argument we are pursuing here is available only to a deontologist who thinks that there could be exceptions to the requirement never to do or permit evil that good may come of it or that sometimes the end will justify the means. An absolute deon-

tologist would summarily reject this line of argument and therefore would immediately be led to the conclusion that God does not exist. Here I am assuming that the absolute deontologist is mistaken about this. Later, however, I will base my argument on specific moral requirements that are acceptable to both consequentialist and deontologists alike, including absolute deontologists.

26. Of course, there is a sense in which God by preventing a first assault would be preventing a second one as well by thus rendering it logically impossible, given the absence of the first assault.

27. Nor would it do to claim that in all the cases where we are assuming that it is logically impossible for God to prevent both morally evil consequences, it could be logically impossible, and not just causally impossible, for us to prevent them as well, because that would still render God impossibly no more powerful than ourselves.

28. Actually, it is God's permission of B that is logically entailed, but God's permission of B in the relevant sense here further entails that B occurs.

29. If there is no action at all in this case, there could be no moral evil consequences either because such consequences are logically tied to free actions.

30. In the latter case, God logically could not prevent the evil consequences of the other action because in that case God would either not be acting freely or not acting at all, and so logically could not be (freely) permitting evil.

31. While the argument here ranges over God and ourselves, it can be generalized to range over God and all other rational moral agents.

32. It is worth pointing out here that in cases of this sort, God's abiding by the Pauline Principle, unlike our own abiding by it, does not involve the loss of overall good consequences. In cases of this sort, God would always have ways of securing good consequences overall without violating the principle.

33. I am ignoring the consequences of evil acts directed against God because God could always prevent such consequences if he wanted to do so and because such consequences couldn't harm God in the sense of harm I have been employing and so would not be horrendously or even significantly evil.

34. There are also other goods to which we have a right in our world, such as compensation for serious assault. However, no one would have to be provided with such goods if God existed, because, God would have always prevented, as needed, the violation of rights that in our world require the provision of such goods.

35. Now there are actions, such as riding a bicycle, that may be only causally impossible for us to do that would be logically impossible for God to do. Nevertheless, such logical impossibilities would not constitute defects or imperfections in God, as would be the case if God were logically incapable of preventing the consequences of horrendously evil actions when we are only at best only causally incapable of preventing them. There is no perfection of God that would explain why he can't prevent the horrendous evil consequences of our immoral actions as there is a perfection of God—his being a pure spirit—that explains why he can't ride a bicycle. So allowing that God is imperfect in this way would be just as bad as allowing that God is less powerful than we are. We would no longer be talking about the God of traditional theism.

36. Thus, having shown that God could not logically be required to permit the consequences of a significant and especially a horrendous rights violation to prevent the consequences of another such rights violation because he could always prevent both consequences, it remains to be seen whether God could logically only provide us a good to which we are not entitled by permitting the consequences of a significant and especially a horrendous rights violation to be inflicted on us or whether God would always have other morally unobjectionably ways of providing us with such goods.

37. The good here is understood to be one to which we are entitled against all possible providers.

38. Still, it might be objected that this is not a case of God permitting evil that an additional good may come of it but rather a case of God permitting evil to prevent a greater evil. The greater evil being prevented here is that of Joseph's extended family being deprived of their basic welfare by the famine. Yet on this reading, not only is Joseph's extended family in need of God's assistance but everyone else as well who is suffering from the famine could also press a similar claim against God. This seems right, but it is also arguable that God in addition to providing basic welfare is also offering Joseph's extended family a special role in the divine plan for making the heavenly afterlife more available, maybe even ultimately available to all, and this is something they certainly could not lay claim as a right.

39. An interesting variant is the Exodus story of Moses and the plagues. In this story, God is said to go further and actually do, not just permit, significant moral evil that good may come of it. Still, here, we do get some account of the moral good that purportedly justifies God actually doing moral evil. In the *New Testament*, the life of Jesus is also presented

as a case where God allows significant evil to bring about a good that we would not otherwise be entitled to have. So this too does have the form of a justified exception to the Pauline Principle. The relevant difference, as we noted earlier, is that Jesus willingly accepts the unjust suffering and death imposed on him whereas no such willing acceptance, or informed consent, is to be found in the overwhelming number of the cases where God would be permitting significant and even horrendous evil consequences of immoral actions, at least at the time God would be permitting those consequences.

40. J.L. Shellenberg and I agree about this. See Shellenberg (2007, Chapter 1). Where we differ is that I employ more of our moral and political knowledge than Schellenberg does to make my argument.

41. I am using "us" here collectively as well as individually.

42. We cannot have a right to be provided with a heavenly afterlife. Nor can we deserve it either. That is too strong a claim as well. Nor could we do anything that would make us worthy of the heavenly afterlife. But through virtuous behavior and through using well whatever opportunities God provides us with for soul-making, we could do what we could be reasonably expected to do to make ourselves less unworthy of a heavenly afterlife. Yet even if we would do all that we can reasonably expected to do to make ourselves less unworthy of a heavenly afterlife, according to Christian orthodoxy, we still would not be worthy of a heavenly afterlife, just further along a continuum.

43. J.L. Schellenberg maintains that even if we do not freely choose to be related to God, say, in friendship, God can and should use his power to establish such a relationship, and furthermore that God's failure to do so logically demonstrates that an all-good, all-powerful God does not exist. See Schellenberg (2007, pp. 267–269). My view is that friendship with God should always be something freely entered into both by God and by ourselves. So there is nothing contradictory for me in God's permitting people not to choose friendship with the Godhead. What is contradictory for me is God's not preventing significant and especially horrendous evil consequences of immoral actions when he can easily do so without sacrificing anything to which we have a right. Moreover, earlier in the same chapter, Schellenberg maintains that the existence of God is logically incompatible with the horrific suffering in our world because God, he assumes, could have made creatures different from us who would "freely" welcome his friendship without having first suffered from such

evils. Yet even if this claim were true under some understanding of free-dom, it would not show that God, if he existed, would be acting wrongly in permitting *us*, given the creatures we are, to suffer horrific evils in the actual world, as the standard argument from evil had attempted to do. By contrast, my argument against the existence of God purports to do just that.

44. This, of course, holds for those who are capable, given the opportunity, of doing what we could be reasonably expected to do to make themselves less unworthy of such a life through soul-making. For those who lack such a capacity something else may be morally appropriate.

45. Of course, soul-making can occur where people's rights have been sig-nificantly violated. In fact, rights violations can provide new occasions for soul-making. Yet a just and powerful political state would try to ensure that the soul-making went on under conditions where justice generally obtains, such that as much as possible its citizens rarely suffered from significant and especially horrendously evil consequences of immoral actions. So, at least initially, I want to focus on the resources available and needed for soul-making under just such ideal conditions.

46. Someone might object here that omitting to provide something does not violate anyone's rights only commissions (interferences) do. Yet even if one accepts this libertarian view, I have argued elsewhere that you can always find a counterpart commission to the more apparent omission if you look more closely at how people are related to each other. See Sterba (2014, Chapter 6).

47. There would be a limit if at some point God started to prevent, rather than permit significant or horrendous evil consequences of immoral actions. Presumably, we would have been able to discern if and when that had begun to happen.

48. Alvin Plantinga has suggested that our opportunity for soul-making might be dependent on human wrongdoing, a view also suggested by the Roman Catholic Easter "felix culpa" liturgy. See Plantinga (2004).

   Now clearly it is part of the Christian redemptive story that the oppor-tunity for heavenly communion with God, including the beatific vision, only came after sin had entered the world. What is primarily at issue here is whether God would not, or even could not, have provided us with such a gift unless the consequences of (significant and even horrendous) sin had entered the world. To claim that the consequences of (significant and even horrendous) sin had to enter the world before God could pro-vide us with the Godly opportunity to make ourselves less unworthy of a heavenly afterlife, however, is clearly morally objectionable. It is morally objectionable for the same reasons that I gave in the text for thinking that God's permission of significant and especially horrendously evil consequences of immoral actions is necessary for the provision of a Godly opportunity for soul-making is morally objectionable. This is because it would foster perverse moral incentives in ourselves and in God as well. In fact, it is just this same kind of perverse thinking that St. Paul was condemning among the Romans when he formulated what has come to be called the Pauline Principle—Never do evil that good may come of it. See Romans (3:5–18). See also Diller (2008, pp. 87–101). I am also assuming here that according to this felix culpa theodicy, the sin that would have had to enter the world before God could provide us with a Godly opportunity for soul-making could not be just the consequences of the original sin of our first ancestors. It would also have to include all the significant and especially the horrendous evil consequences of immoral actions of all of us, past, present, and future. If it did not include those evil consequences, there would be no justification for God's permitting, rather than preventing, them. But if it does include them, then, as I argued, we face the problem that it would give rise to perverse moral incentives for us and for God. Hence, a felix culpa theodicy should be rejected on this account.

49. While I have chosen to put my argument in terms of goods to which we have a right and goods to which we do not have a right, I could have put it in terms of goods that others have an obligation or a duty to provide us with and goods that others do not have obligation or duty to provide us with. It would have just been a bit more cumbersome to put my argument in this other way.

50. I earlier argued that with respect to permitting the consequences of horrendous evil action in order to prevent a greater evil, it is always possible for God to prevent both evils, whereas when we are in a comparable situation, we cannot always prevent both evils because of our limited causal powers. Accordingly, what we should do in such contexts is not prevent the lesser evil in order to prevent the greater evil. In so acting, we still would be acting justly and not violating anyone's rights because we lack the causal power to prevent both evils and "ought" requires "can" here. However, things are different for God. If God, who is all-powerful, were not to prevent both evils in my example, he would not be acting justly and he would be violating the rights of at least one of the children.

51. When I refer to anyone's rights or having a right, I mean to be referring to conclusive, first-order rights which imply that these rights have not been forfeited. When I refer to not having a right, I mean to refer to not having even a prima facie, first-order right.

52. Securing the liberty to which one is entitled may sometimes involve interfering with the liberty of someone else, but not interfering with a liberty to which that person is entitled, as when the police in a just society stop (interfere with the liberty) of someone trying to steal your car. Furthermore, that to which we have a conclusive right cannot be in conflict with that to which anyone else has a conclusive right.

53. While I will argue here that it is not logically impossible for God to both provide us with a Godly opportunity for soul-making, something to which we have no right and to prevent horrendous evil consequences of immoral actions from being inflicted on us, something to which we do have a right, it would be logically impossible for God to provide us with certain goods to which we have no right, such as an opportunity to console a rape victim, without having previously permitted certain related rights to be violated, as by allowing a person to be raped. Yet, just as you or I would not be justified in allowing someone to be raped in order to provide someone with the opportunity to console a rape victim, I contend that neither would God be justified in permitting such actions to be done. Notice too that both the rape victim and whomever would receive the opportunity to console the rape victim would morally prefer that God had prevented the rape and instead had provided other opportunities for soul-making that would not violate anyone conclusive moral rights.

54. In the latter case, God could not choose to provide us with a Godly opportunity for soul-making because in that case God would either not be acting freely or not acting at all.

55. Sometimes I am assuming a conclusive right as here. At under times, as in the next sentence, I am assuming just a prima facie right.

56. Supererogatory goods are goods we ought to provide to others even though we are not required to do so. So while a Godly opportunity for soul-making is a gift and something that is good for us, it would be too strong to say that God ought to provide us with this opportunity. So the provision of this opportunity by God goes beyond supererogation because there is no sense according to which God ought to provide this opportunity, although it is a good thing when he does.

57. In *The Acts of the Apostles*, at an important gathering of the early Christians, Peter begins by affirming the universality of salvation: "Now I understand that God is not a respecter of persons, but that in every nation he who fears him and does what is right is acceptable to him" (Acts 10:34).

58. This follows from the fact that God is logically unconstrained with respect to the provision of such opportunities unless he is impossibly less powerful than ourselves. It also should be pointed out here that in cases of this sort, God's abiding by the Pauline Principle, unlike our own abiding by it, does not involve the loss of overall good consequences. In cases of this sort, God would always have ways of securing good consequences overall without violating the principle.

59. There may be some limit on the resources that God could provide to humans in cases where doing so would come into conflict with the basic needs of nonhuman living beings. Here a solution to the problem of natural evil would be needed.

60. Here the example focuses on what is usually thought of as doing good rather than preventing evil, even though it really still is a case of preventing evil.

61. To complicate things here a bit, maybe even in this case, God's intervention should not be completely successful. This is because if we discovered that only when we intervened ourselves, really doing our best, was the intervention completely successful, that could motivate us to always do our best, relying on God for help only when we could do no more ourselves.

62. I argued for this restriction in section VI of this chapter.

63. This is the sort of objection that Peter Van Inwagen raises in defense of theism in his *The Problem of Evil* (van Inwagen 2006, Lecture 5). Another counter to this objection is that those who would only turn to God after he had permitted them to suffer unjustly would not be displaying an appropriate moral character. An appropriate moral character would display a willingness to turn to God in a wide variety of contexts. It would display a willingness to do all that can be done to make oneself less unworthy of a heavenly afterlife.

64. Now it might be objected that God did show himself benevolent and protective to our first parents, Adam and Eve, and that only when they disobeyed him did God begin punishing them and their descendants. Yet despite the fact that our first ancestors would have been incapable of harming God so that the first significant wrongful actions had to be directed at our fellow creatures not at God, the idea that we would be

morally responsible for the significant wrongs that our prehistoric ancestors committed against each other is repugnant to our morality and so should be to God's as well. At some point the accountability for the effects of the wrongdoing of our ancestors has to wash away. Clearly, 200,000 years is way beyond the limit.

65. It might be questioned whether this is really a logical argument from evil. See Bishop and Perszyk (2011, pp. 109–126). However, if we are dealing with nonoptional requirements of morality, as I think we are, then an omni-God, if such a God exists, would be clearly involved in the widespread prevention of significant and especially horrendous evil consequences of immoral actions and involved in the widespread provision of basic goods to those who has a right to those goods. But this obviously has not happened. Hence, our nonoptional morality and these widespread morally objectionable outcomes are logically incompatible with the existence of an omni-God. In their article, Bishop and Perszyk almost come to recognize this as well.

66. This is assuming that the point of the discussion here is in some way or other to advance the case for theism or for atheism.

67. Actually, Bergmann's skeptical argument can only succeed in defending theism against even a probabilistic argument from evil by mistakenly assuming that we are more ignorant than we, in fact, are, as I have shown in this chapter.

68. It is worth pointing out here that in cases of this sort, God's abiding by this constraint, unlike our own abiding by it, does not involve the loss of overall good consequences. This is because God would always have ways of securing good consequences overall without violating the constraint.

69. This is also something that superheroes almost always do as well in our imagination.

70. See Bergmann (2014, p. 214). See also Bergmann (2001, pp. 282, 284–286).

71. Nevertheless, although I am willing to appeal to tenets of Christian orthodoxy whenever I can, I believe that my argument does not rest on them, but can work quite effectively just using the requirements from ordinary morality such as the distinction between that to which we have a right to and that to which we don't have a right, and, of course, the Pauline Principle and its Kantian analogues. In fact, my argument, as we shall see, can rest on even weaker moral requirements than these, which, as I shall show, makes my argument even stronger.

72. Note that providing such a good would also be preventing an evil.

Bibliography

Adams, Marilyn. 1999. *Horrendous Evils and the Goodness of God*. Ithaca: Cornell University Press.

Bergmann, Michael. 1999. Might-Counterfactuals, Transworld Untrustworthiness and Plantinga's Free Will Defense. *Faith and Philosophy* 16 (3): 336–351.

———. 2001. Skeptical Theism and Rowe's New Evidential Argument from Evil. *Nous* 35: 278–296.

———. 2009. Skeptical Theism and the Problem of Evil. In *Flint, Thomas and Rea, Michael, Oxford Handbook of Philosophical Theology*, 375–399. Oxford: Oxford University Press.

———. 2012. Commonsense Skeptical Theism. In *Reason, Metaphysics and Mind: New Essays on the Philosophy of Alvin Plantinga*, ed. K. Clark and M. Rea. New York: Oxford University Press.

———. 2014. Skeptical Theism, Atheism and Total Evidence Skepticism. In *Skeptical Theism: New Essays*, ed. Trent Dougherty and Justin McBrayer, 209–220. Oxford: Oxford University Press.

Bergmann, Michael, and Michael Rea. 2005. In Defense of Skeptical Theism: A Reply to Almeida and Oppy. *Australasian Journal of Philosophy* 83: 241–251.

Bergmann, Michael, Michael Murray, and Michael Rea, eds. 2011. *Divine Evil? The Moral Character of the God of Abraham*. Oxford: Oxford University Press.

Bishop, John, and Ken Perszyk. 2011. The Normatively Relativized Logical Argument from Evil. *International Journal of Philosophy of Religion* 70: 109–126.

Boer, Steven. 1978. The Irrelevance of the Free Will Defense. *Analysis* 38 (3): 110–112.

Buchanan, Alan, and Dan Brock. 1989. *Deciding for Others: The Ethics of Surrogate Decision-Making*. Cambridge: Cambridge University Press.

Coughlan, Michael. 1979. Moral Evil Without Consequences. *Analysis* 39: 58–60.

Diller, Kevin. 2008. Are Sin and Evil Necessary for a Really Good World? Questions for Alvin Plantinga's Felix Culpa Theodicy. *Faith and Philosophy* 25: 87–101.

Dilley, Frank. 1982. Is the Free Will Defense Irrelevant? *Religious Studies* 18: 355–364.

Dostoyevsky, Fyodor. 1966. *Brothers Karamazov*. New York: Airmont Publishing Co.

Draper, P. 1996. The Skeptical Theist. In *The Evidential Argument from Evil*, ed. Daniel Howard-Snyder, 175–192. Bloomington: Indiana University Press.

———. 2009. The Problem of Evil. In *The Oxford Handbook of Philosophical Theology*, ed. Thomas P. Flint and Michael Rea. Oxford: Oxford University Press.

Faden, Ruth, and Tom L. Beauchamp. 1986. *A History and Theory of Informed Consent*. New York: Oxford University Press.

Finnis, John. 1991. *Moral Absolutes: Tradition, Revision and Truth*. Washington, DC: Catholic University of America.

Howard-Snyder, Daniel. 2009. Epistemic Humility, Arguments from Evil, and Moral Skepticism. In *Oxford Studies in Philosophy of Religion*, ed. J. Kvanvig, 2. Oxford: Oxford University Press.

———. 2013. The Argument from Inscrutable Evil. In *The Evidential Argument from Evil*, 286–310. Bloomington: Indiana University Press.

McKim, Robert. 1984. Worlds Without Evil. *International Journal of Philosophy of Religion* 15: 164–170.

O'Neill, Onora. 2002. *Autonomy and Trust in Bioethics*. Cambridge: Cambridge University Press.

Plantinga, Alvin. 1974. *The Nature of Necessity*. Oxford: Clarendon Press.

———. 2004. Supralapsarianism. Or 'O Felix Culpa'. In *Christian Faith and the Problem of Evil*, ed. Peter van Inwagen. Grand Rapids: Eerdmans.

Schellenberg, J.L. 2007. *The Wisdom to Doubt*. Ithaca: Cornell University Press.

Sterba, James P. 2005. *The Triumph of Practice Over Theory in Ethics*. New York: Oxford University Press.

———. 2014. *From Rationality to Equality*. Oxford: Oxford University Press.

van Inwagen, P. 1988. The Magnitude, Duration, and Distribution of Evil: A Theodicy. *Philosophical Topics* 16: 161–187.

———. 2006. *The Problem of Evil*. Oxford: Oxford University Press.

Wykstra, S. 1984. The Human Obstacle to Evidential Arguments from Suffering: On Avoiding the Evils of 'Appearance'. *International Journal of Philosophy of Religion* 16: 73–84.

———. 1996. Rowe's Noseeum Arguments from Evil. In *The Evidential Argument from Evil*, ed. D. Howard-Snyder, 126–150. Bloomington: Indiana University Press.

Wykstra, S. with Timothy Perrine. 2012. Foundations of Skeptical Theism. *Faith and Philosophy* 29: 375–399.

6

What If God Is Not a Moral Agent?

Skeptical theists all start out with the assumption that God is a moral agent and seek to show how it is logically possible for God's permission of all the evil in the world to be morally justified. In the previous chapter, I too assumed that God is a moral agent and argued that the skeptical theist argument fails primarily because the existence of God is logically incompatible with fundamental requirements of our morality. Yet suppose one were to drop the assumption that God is a moral agent, would that help support the case for theism? Among contemporary philosophers of religion, Brian Davies is probably best known for his attempt to use the work of Thomas Aquinas to defend theism in just this way. So it is important to consider his Thomistic approach to the problem of evil.

I

According to Davies, if Aquinas is right then the problem of evil as it is usually understood by contemporary philosophers of religion "is not a serious problem at all but rather the result of a confused way of thinking about God" (Davies 2011) As Davies sees it, this is because for Aquinas

© The Author(s) 2019
J. P. Sterba, *Is a Good God Logically Possible?*,
https://doi.org/10.1007/978-3-030-05469-4_6

there is no need to morally justify God's behavior toward us. "God is not to be thought of a moral agent behaving well or badly" (Ibid., p. 114): to do so is simply a "category mistake" (Davies 2006, p. 103).

As Davies puts it,

> We cannot think of God as possessing human virtues, which as Aristotle notes, are dispositions needed by people in order to flourish as people (albeit that our possession of virtue might bring us to our graves). Nor can we think of God as being obligated in any intelligible sense. In this sense, it would be wrong to think of God's goodness as a matter of conforming to some standard to which he is subject. To do that would be to forget about the difference there must be between creatures and God. (Davies 2011, p. 117)

Now the language of moral virtue and moral obligation is usually not thought to apply to God in exactly the same way it applies to us. Most of us experience a struggle to be morally virtuous, sometimes making progress sometimes not, doing well with respect to some virtues, doing not so well with respect to others. Similarly, with regard to moral obligation. We can recognize the pull of moral obligations while also being pulled in other directions, and, as a result, we sometimes end up doing what we clearly know to be wrong. However, it is usually understood to be different for God. God, it is thought, could be morally virtuous and fulfill his moral obligations to us without the struggle we experience.

Yet here Davies disagrees. While he admits that the language of virtue does apply to God, he denies that moral virtue is what is at stake.[1] Nevertheless, the virtue of justice as applied to God does present a significant challenge for Davies's view. As Davies sees it, divine justice is giving everyone what is owing to them according to God's plan (Davies 2011, p. 63 quoting Aquinas). To say that God is just simply amounts to God's giving his creatures what is owed to them, "given the natures that they have as his creatures (natures of his own making and design)" (Ibid., p. 117). For Davies, this seems to involve simply sustaining them in existence, not interfering with or aiding them in the world in any way. Here Davies, following Aquinas, appeals to a parent analogy to support his view of how God is just (Ibid., p. 63). Parents do not owe a debt to their children and so being just to them is not a way of repaying a debt. Instead, parents are just toward their children by providing for their needs and by protecting them from danger as far as they can. Nevertheless, parents who did no more than merely sustain their children in existence would hardly be considered just. So judged by Davies's own parent analogy, it would seem that a God who simply did no more for us than sustain us in existence could not be considered just. But then after first endorsing the parent analogy, Davies backs away from it. As he puts it, God's loving us as a father loves his children must ultimately be understood metaphorically.[2] For Davies, what we can literally attribute to God is that he brings us into existence and sustains us there. From which he infers that all talk of God intervening, as parents might to help their children, has to be understood metaphorically.[3]

According to Davies, God can intervene only by entering into a situation from which he is first absent, and God cannot be thought to be absent from anything he creates (Davies 2006, p. 75). Nevertheless, Davies does allow that miracles, which are commonly taken to be examples of divine interventions, can be understood to be part of God's initial (presumably noninterventionist) act of creation (Ibid., p. 76). So it turns out that Davies really does allow that it is possible for God to intervene in human history as long as those interventions are also understood to be bundled into God's initial act of creation.

II

It might be thought that rather than trying to reconcile God with the evil found in the world, as Davies does, by denying that moral virtues apply to God, it might be preferable to adopt a pure divine command theory of morality.[4] Such a theory maintains that things are right or wrong simply on the basis of the commands of God. But then it would not be possible to use morality to challenge the existence of God because according to divine command theory, without God and his commands, there would be no morality. Thus, under divine command theory, the problem of evil cannot even get started.[5]

Now divine command theory has long been discussed by philosophers at least since the time of Plato. In the *Euthyphro*, Socrates argues in favor of the opposing view that God commands things because they are right and hence that morality is fundamentally independent of religion in a way that even God, assuming there is a God, would have to affirm. Still others, however, have endorsed a divine command theory of morality.[6]

Nevertheless, there are serious problems with a divine command theory. One is how are we to understand God's commands. Thus, suppose we had a list of God's commands, how should we understand them? We might think of God as a one-person legislature with ourselves having a role analogous to the judiciary and executive branches of government. God as the one-person legislature would make the commands/laws, and we, as the judiciary/executive, would have the task of interpreting and applying them.

There would be differences, however. The U.S. judiciary in interpreting the laws often tries to determine what purpose the legislature had in passing a particular law, and whether that purpose accords with the U.S. Constitution. And sometimes the US judiciary strikes down laws passed by the legislature as unconstitutional.

According to divine command theory, however, there would be no comparable role for humans to have with respect to the commands of God. We couldn't, for example, strike down any of God's commands because they failed to accord with some independent moral standard. Thus, our role in interpreting and applying God's commands under divine command theory would be narrowly circumscribed. Even so, there are further problems understanding what that role would be.

This is because divine commands could, presumably, come into conflict. Thus, suppose we had one divine command that we should each love and care for the members of our family and another that we should love and care for the deserving poor. Surely, these two commands would conflict when we are faced with the option of using our limited resources to either provide luxuries for the members of our family or use those same resources to provide for the basic needs of the deserving poor. Here we seem to require some kind of a background theory that compares the good that would be accomplished in each case as well as weighs the competing obligations involved, and then makes a recommendation about what should be done.

Yet divine command theory provides no such background theory for resolving conflicts between commands. Under the theory, each command is obligatory simply because it is commanded by God. Conflicts that arise among God's commands could be appropriately resolved only by yet another command of God that shows which command has priority. This is because, according to divine command theory, the resolution of conflicts always could go either way. So there is no way for us to figure out, in advance, how it should go. This then would leave us with only a very minimal role when interpreting or applying the commands of God, and in cases where those commands conflict, we would be at a complete loss as to what to do.

Another problem with divine command theory is determining what God has actually commanded to us do. It would seem that divine command theorists maintain that God's commands are received through special revelations to particular individuals or groups. But if the commands of God are made known only to a few, how can others know what those commands are or when they are reasonably bound to obey them? Presumably, people can only be morally bound by commands they know about and have reason to accept.

To add a further complication, different individuals and groups have claimed to be recipients of special revelations that conflict in ways which would support conflicting moral requirements. Of course, if some of those who claim to have received a special revelation rise to power, they may be able to force obedience on the rest. But then others would have no independent reason to go along with that forceful imposition.

Probably the most serious problem with divine command theory is that just anything could turn out to be the right thing to do, such as torturing babies for the fun of it, depending on the sheer commands of God. But the idea that just anything could turn out to be the right thing to do, irrespective of how harmful it is to human beings has been widely seen by theists and atheists alike to be sufficient to defeat the view.

III

Happily, Davies does not favor a divine command theory approach to the problem of evil.[7] Rather, he contends that what is good for us depends on the way God has made us. It thus depends on, paraphrasing St. Paul, abiding by the law of reason God embedded in our hearts (Romans 2:14–16). As Davies puts it, "God could never command us to torture children because in effect that would involve him in contradicting himself, or going against his nature as the source of creaturely goodness (the nature of which … we can determine, at least to a large extent, independently of theological reflection)" (Davies 2009, p. 122). This seems right.

However, if God cannot command us to do anything that goes against the law of reason that he embedded in our hearts because that would involve God in a contradiction, then, it would also seem that God could not act against that same law of reason that he embedded in our hearts because that too would involve God in a contradiction. Thus, God, for example, like us, would be required not to torture children. But Davies rejects this result on the grounds that it would make God a moral agent with moral requirements or obligations like ourselves.

How can Davies hold this? If it would be contradictory for God to implant a law in our nature that applies to all rational agents and then command that we act against it, why would it not also be contradictory for God to implant a law in our nature that applies to all rational agents and command us not to act against it, while at the same time regularly acting against the law himself in his dealings with us?[8] Clearly, if the first set of actions involves God in a contradiction, the second set of actions should do so as well. This is because the law of nature that God presumably implanted in our hearts is understood to apply to all rational beings including God himself. So it would indeed be contradictory for God to implant a law of nature in our hearts that applies to himself and then to act contrary to that very law that he promulgated.[9]

Of course, it is possible for Davies to avoid contradiction here by retreating to a divine command theory. But Davies doesn't want to go there. This means that he is committed to the idea of God implanting a law of nature in our hearts which applies to all rational agents including himself, commanding us to abide by that law, especially its requirement not to inflict significant and especially horrendous harm on others (that can be easily avoided), and thus to God's being committed to abiding by that requirement himself. That does make God a moral agent, like ourselves, but one with the power and knowledge to surely get things right. So the idea that God is a moral agent subject to moral requirements is not an auxiliary assumption that Davies could just excise from his view. Rather, it is a consequence of the fundamental assumptions about God and morality that Davies himself endorses.

Yet even if Davies were to find a defensible way to drop the assumptions he makes about God and morality, it is not clear in what sense he wants to maintain that God is not subject to moral requirements. Clearly, sometimes we are not subject to moral requirements because we lack the capacity to recognize to them and sometimes we are not subject to certain moral requirements while we are subject to others, but neither of these ways of not being subject to moral requirements could apply to God. Nor would it do to say that God is not subject to moral requirements in an obligatory sense but is subject to them in a supererogatory one. For example, this would imply that while God morally ought to have prevented the horrendous evil consequences of the Holocaust, he was just not blameworthy for failing to do so. But that cannot be right.[10]

This suggests that the real problem with Davies account is not so much with his denial that God is subject to moral requirements. Rather, the real problem is that God, if he exists, and were not subject to such requirements, would still admittedly be permitting the horrendous evil consequences of all the immoral actions in the world when he could easily have prevented them without either permitting a greater evil or failing to secure a greater good, which is far more evil than that has been produced by all the great villains among us.[11] That is the real problem.

IV

Yet even if Davies were to find a defensible way of showing that God is not subject to moral requirements, he still would need to find a way to characterize God as good in some other way than being morally good. So it is important that he tries to establish that result with the following argument:

1. All things seek their good (that which attracts).
2. All things seeking their good are effects of God (things made to be by God).
3. Effects are somehow like their causes.
4. Therefore, the goodness which creatures are drawn to is like God who can therefore be thought of as attractive (or good) like the goods to which creatures are attracted. (Davies 2006, p. 163)

However, there are problems with this argument. Concerning (1), the idea that all things, not just living things, seek their good belongs to an Aristotelian worldview that is no longer credible today.[12] Still, we can allow premise (1) if we limit its domain to just living beings.[13] Premise (2) then becomes

(2′) All living things seeking their good are effects of God.

We can then accept (2′) for the sake of argument. Premise (3), however, is challenged by the countless examples that modern science provides of the emergence of greater physical complexity or higher forms of life from simpler beginnings. And even if we endorsed a weaker version of (3), it is hard to see how we could still derive (4). Right off, it would seem that we the most we could hope to derive is

(4′) God, like the living things he causes, seeks his own good.

Moreover, given that (4′) would be based on evidence such as:

> Hitler sought his own good
> Mother Theresa sought her own good
> Stalin sought his own good,

it is not at all clear how we should interpret the claim that God seeks his own good. Still, Davies wants to focus on the goods that all living beings seek and infer from God being the cause of all living beings each seeking its good, that God must be like the goods that all these beings seek. But given that the goods that living beings seek include:

1) natural goods that are taken to be good as ends
2) natural evils that are taken to be good as means
3) moral goods that are taken to be good as ends
4) moral evils that are taken to be good as means,

how would it help to know that God is like this large collection of natural and moral goods and evils? More to the point, how would knowing this enable us to infer that God is good in some useful nonmoral sense?

V

Yet maybe there is another way for Davies to get closer to the conclusion he wants. Even if it cannot be reached by exploring God's causal connection to the goods living beings actually do seek, maybe it can still be reached by showing that God is not causally connected in any problematic way to the evil that is present in the world. In any case, that is a line of argument that Davies does pursue (Davies 2006, Chapter 7 and Davies 2011, Chapter 7).

Davies begins by distinguishing two kinds of evil, malum poenae, literally evil of punishment, or what Davies likes to call evil suffered, and malum culpae or evil of fault, which Davies likes to call evil done. Evils suffered are natural evils while evils done are moral evils, and God's relationship to each is said to be different. What is common, Davies claims, is that God never directly wills or causes any evil as an end itself. Now this might sound like a useful way of distinguishing between God and evildoers, but it turns out to be of no use at all. This is because, as Aquinas makes clear, no agent directly wills or causes any evil as an end itself. All agents, whether natural or moral evil is at stake, never will or cause any evil as an end in itself but only as a means to some good. All agents, Aquinas maintains, following Aristotle here, whether they are good or bad, always act to bring about what they perceive to be good.[14]

Nevertheless, even granting this, there is still the question of whether we can relevantly distinguish natural evils from moral evils. Now Davies thinks that we can. With respect to evils suffered, God is said to will these evils indirectly as a means to some good. For example, God can will the zebra's demise to bring about the lion's survival. With respect to evils done, however, things are different. Here Davies maintains God cannot will the evil done, even indirectly (because there is no good to which it could be a means) (Davies 2011, pp. 70–71).

So can this way of distinguishing God's relationship to evils suffered and evils done provide Davies with a way of characterizing God as good in some nonmoral sense? Here Davies thinks he can minimize God's involvement with moral evil by claiming that God only causes the sinner's action, which insofar as it exists is good, but not the sinner's sin which is a privation (Davies 2006, p. 97). But if this exonerates God from responsibility for the moral evil in the world, it exonerates sinners as well. This is because we could also claim that sinners cause their own actions, and insofar as those actions exist, they are good, and that sin is just a privation of moral goodness in their acts. That privation is simply a byproduct or a means of achieving the good toward which their acts are directed. It is not something that sinners ultimately will or cause. Given then that we can provide parallel accounts of God's and sinners' relationship to moral evil, we have no reason for not morally evaluating them both. Hence, we need to give up any claim that we are aiming to characterize God as good in some acceptable nonmoral sense. Rather, what is at stake is whether given what we know about God's relationship to natural and moral evil in the world, we can still think of God as morally good.

VI

As it turns out, in pursuing an answer to this question, Davies provides some useful examples:

> Suppose that you go for a walk down a country lane in winter with a strong wind blowing. The wind causes a branch of a tree to break. The branch crashes onto you and you end up dead.

Again, suppose that you go for a walk down a country lane in winter with a strong wind blowing. This time, however, I am lurking with a branch, I crash it onto you, and you end up dead.

Davies goes on to explain the relevant difference between the two cases:

When it comes to consequences, we have identical scenarios here: you dead by virtue of a branch hitting you. Morally speaking, however, we have totally different situations. In one, there is no moral evil. In the other, there is. And the difference lies in the fact that one scenario is intended by someone. It is the intention to do wrong (or intention to refuse to aim for some good for which one should strive) that constitutes moral badness or evil. In this sense, moral badness lies only in individual agents and not in the effects of their actions. (Ibid., pp. 175–176)

So Davies's examples are supposed to help us understand how God would not be causing anything in the case of moral evil. Moral evil is said to consist in a wrongful intention or the refusal to aim at some good. The consequences of this inner act are said not to be part of the moral evil or the evil done. So this would imply that these consequences would have to be just evil suffered.

This opens up two possibilities for Davies. First, the evil suffered could be related to God the way all other evils suffered are said to be related to God—they could be indirectly caused by God to achieve some appropriate good. Second, the evil suffered could just lack any further good for which God would be willing it as a means.

The first possibility, the one that Davies does not favor, suggests that the consequences of moral evil could be justified in the very same way natural evil is said to be justified. But then God would be related to the consequences of moral evil in the same way he is related to natural evil with the result that the same accepting relationship God is said to have toward natural evil would be transferred to the consequences of moral evil.

This is a troubling result, however, because there is a fundamental difference between natural evil and the consequences of moral evil. Thus, with respect to natural evil in our world, it is not possible to avoid all significant natural evil. When a wolf and a deer are seriously in conflict in our world, either the wolf will survive or the deer will survive. One or the other will suffer death.[15] However, with respect to the consequences of moral evil, especially the horrendous evil sort, the situation is different. Except for lifeboat cases, individual human beings are not in unavoidable life-and-death conflict with each other. With respect to most of the conflicts we have, morality imposes its demands on each of us such that it is possible for us all to live decent lives together, without anyone doing anything that imposes especially horrendously morally evil consequences on anyone else. This is why it would be possible for God to prevent all the significant and especially the horrendous evil consequences of our immoral actions, as needed, at the same time that it would not be possible, to prevent all the significant or even the horrendous evil consequences of natural evil in the world. Hence, it would be morally objectionable to treat the consequences of moral evil as justifiable in the same way that natural evil is justifiable.

The second possibility, the one that Davies actually favors, does not face the same objection as the first. The second possibility maintains that the evil suffered could just lack any further good for which God would be willing it as a means. The problem with this possibility is that if God is not willing the consequences of immoral action, especially horrendously immoral actions, as a means to some further good, why then is he permitting them? Put another way, how could God permit the consequences of immoral actions, especially the horrendously evil consequences, while admitting that there is no good in virtue of which those consequences could be justified as a means? If there is no good that could justify God's permission of the consequences of immoral actions, then God should not be permitting those consequences. Instead, he should be preventing them, which unfortunately has not been happening.

There is a further problem with Davies's account of moral evil itself (Davies 2006, pp. 183–190). Even if moral evils are just inner acts of misguided intention, as Davies claims, God would not be powerless with respect to them. God could still prevent such acts from obtaining. So we need to ask, why does God not do this? Of course, justifications in terms of freedom are more readily available for such inner acts than for the consequences of those inner acts that affect others. The point is simply that a justification is required for God's permitting rather than preventing even such inner immoral acts; we can't go on as if no justification is required. Nevertheless, it is the lack of any justification for God's permitting the (external) consequences of immoral acts (which Davies claims cannot be a means to any good) that is the most serious problem for Davies's account.

VII

Now there are passages in Aquinas that suggest a different taxonomy of natural and moral evil and a somewhat different justification for them than Davies provides. In the *Summa Theologiae*, Aquinas says that God can indirectly will natural evil as when God (paraphrasing) wills the preservation of the natural by willing that some things be naturally corrupted. As for moral evil, however, Aquinas wants to hold that God does not either will evil to be or will it not to be, but rather God wills to permit it. Yet this can't be right. This is because there are two relevant distinctions here. One is between willing something as an end and willing something as a means. The other is between intending something and merely foreseeing it. So if agents, like ourselves, do something, we either intend a particular consequence of our action or merely foresee that consequence while intending to do something else. There is no other possibility.[16] Further, willing something as an end or willing something as a means are two ways of acting intentionally.

So how does Aquinas's willing directly and willing indirectly relate to these distinctions? I think it is just another way of putting the distinction between willing something as an end and willing something as a means. This seems to fit Aquinas's natural corruption example.

This leads to the crucial question: How does Aquinas's claim that God wills to permit moral evil fit with these distinctions? From the text, Aquinas clearly wants to distinguish it from God's willing natural evil as a means. This might be possible if moral evil were a foreseen, but not an intended, consequence of God's willing. But this cannot be the case because permitting is always an intentional act, never something that is merely a foreseen consequence of something else that is done intentionally. Nor is it clear how God, who, as Davies wants to stress, intentionally causes the reality of everything that exists, could ever be acting in a merely foreseen way. This constitutes a serious problem for Aquinas's account because it implies that in permitting horrendous evil consequences of immoral actions God cannot be simply foreseeing those consequences but rather must be intentionally willing them at least as a means, which Aquinas says God does not do.

VIII

So what should be done to resolve this problem? Clearly, we need to drop opposition to the idea that by permitting a moral evil act and its consequences God would not be willing them as a means to some good. This would open the door to the possibility that there is a greater good justification for God's permitting of both natural and moral evil.[17] Elsewhere, Aquinas himself seem to suggest that he too favors a greater good justification for God's permission of natural and moral evil. Thus, he quotes Augustine approvingly saying: "Since God is supremely powerful and good to bring even good from evil belongs to the limitless goodness of God that he permits evils to exist and draws good from them."[18]

In fact, a greater good justification for God's permission of natural and moral evil is widely held by contemporary theists and atheists alike to be the only conceivable way God could be justified in permitting those evils.[19] However, William Rowe, who himself defends the need for a greater good justification, takes it to be only a necessary not a sufficient condition for justifying God's permission of evil (Rowe 1979, p. 336). Surely for us a greater good justification is not always morally acceptable. Take the often-discussed, hopefully just hypothetical, case of a surgeon who uses the organs of a perfectly healthy person off the street to save the lives of five terminally ill patients.[20] Here the greater good of saving five lives is not thought to justify the means that would have to be used to achieve it.[21] Arguably, seemingly comparable constraints would hold of God as well.[22]

Nevertheless, it is clear that a greater good justification for moral evil does work for a range of cases with regard to us. As I noted in the introduction, these cases can be viewed as justifiable exceptions to the

Pauline Principle's requirement never to do evil that good may come of it. For us, such exceptions can be trivial (as in the case of stepping on someone's foot to get out of a crowded subway) or easily reparable as in the case of lying to a temporarily depressed friend to keep her from committing suicide. There are also exceptions of this sort for us where doing evil is greatly outweighed by the consequences of the action, especially to innocent people (as in the case of shooting one of twenty civilian hostages to prevent, in the only way possible, the execution of all twenty).

Yet are there comparable cases for God? Looking around the world and back through history, there would have to be greater goods to justify especially all the horrendous evil consequences of immoral actions that God would have to be permitting if he exists. So we need to determine whether such greater good justifications can work for God.

IX

In answering this question, I will sometimes be drawing on parts of the arguments from previous chapters. As before, I will be focusing on whether there would be a justification for God's not preventing, hence permitting, the final stage of significant and especially horrendous evil actions of wrongdoers, the stage where the wrongdoers would be imposing their evil consequences on their victims. I am assuming that there would be a justification, at least in terms of freedom, for God's not interfering with the imaginings, intending, and even the taking of initial steps by wrongdoers toward bringing about significant and even horrendous evil consequences on their would-be victims. I am also assuming that there would be a justification, at least in terms of freedom, for God's not interfering when the consequences of immoral actions are not significantly evil. So the question is: Is there a greater good justification for God's permitting significant and especially horrendous evil consequences of immoral actions?

Now it is important to see that goods that could be provided to us are of just two types. Either they are goods to which we have a right or they are goods to which we do not have a right.

Goods to Which We Have a Right

Providing us with goods to which we have a right is also a way of preventing evil. More precisely, the provision of such goods by those who could easily do so without violating anyone's rights is a way of preventing the evil of the violation of people's rights.[23] Thus, if I provide someone with food and lodging to which that person has a right when I alone, other than God, can easily do so, I prevent that person from suffering an evil. Correspondingly, the nonprovision of goods to which we have a right is also a way of doing evil; more precisely, the nonprovision of such goods by those who could easily provide them without violating anyone's rights would itself be morally evil.[24] Thus, if I do not provide someone with the food and lodging to which that person has a right when I alone, other than God, can easily do so, my omission, which is morally equivalent to a doing here, is also morally evil.

In addition, goods to which we are entitled are either first-order goods that do not logically presuppose the existence of some serious wrongdoing (like the freedom from brutal assault) or second-order goods that do logically presuppose the existence of some serious wrongdoing (like coming to the aid of a victim of brutal assault). Now for all such first-order goods to which we are entitled, the basic moral requirement that governs their provision is:

Moral Evil Prevention Requirement I

Prevent, rather than permit, significant and especially horrendous evil consequences of immoral actions without violating anyone's rights (a good to which we have a right) when that can easily be done.[25]

For example, if you can easily prevent a small child from going hungry or aid someone who has been brutally assaulted without violating anyone's rights then you should do so. This requirement is an exceptionless minimal component of the Pauline Principle discussed in previous chapters, which would be acceptable to consequentialists and nonconsequentialists, as well as theists and atheists alike. This requirement would be acceptable to consequentialists and nonconsequentialists alike because as this minimal component of the Pauline Principle has been formulated there are no good consequentialist or nonconsequentialist reasons for violating it.[26] Theists and atheists also accept this requirement for the same reasons that consequentialist and nonconsequentialists accept it. However, theists also believe that God, without violating this requirement, can be morally justified in permitting significant and especially horrendous evil consequences of immoral action in order to prevent greater evil consequences.[27] Atheists would just love to be able to demonstrate that theists are mistaken about this.

First-Order Goods to Which We Have a Right
Now with respect to first-order goods to which we have a right, we are sometimes stuck in a situation where we can only provide some people with such a good and hence prevent a corresponding evil from being inflicted on them by not providing other people with another good whose nonprovision inflicts a lesser evil on them. For example, we may be able to save only five people from being robbed and assaulted if we don't try to also save two other people from being robbed and assaulted who are farther away. God, however, would never find himself causally stuck in such situations. God would always have the causal power to prevent both evils, and it would be contradictory for him to be logically constrained from doing so.[28] Accordingly, this is what God would have to do unless there is a good to which we are not entitled the provision of which would justify God in permitting the lesser evil in such cases.

Second-Order Goods to Which We Have a Right
With respect to second-order goods to which we have a right, such as receiving needed medical aid after being brutally assaulted, of course, it would be wrong not to provide such goods when one can easily do so without violating anyone's rights. However, given that the need we have for such goods depends on the existence of significant moral wrongdoing, it would be morally preferable for anyone who could do so to prevent the consequences of that wrongdoing on which the second-order good depends. This is because the victims of significant moral wrongdoing who would have a second-order right to such goods would have morally preferred that anyone who could have easily done so would have kept them from suffering the consequences of the wrongdoing that would ground their right to any second-order goods of rectification and compensation. For example, a victim of a brutal assault would have morally

preferred that anyone who could have easily done so would have prevented the consequences of his assault to his now having the right to second-order goods resulting from that assault. So we have:

Moral Evil Prevention Requirement II

Do not permit, rather than prevent, significant and especially horrendous evil consequences of immoral actions simply to provide other rational beings with goods they would morally prefer not to have.

This requirement too is an exceptionless minimal component of the Pauline Principle which would be acceptable to consequentialists and nonconsequentialists and it should be acceptable to theists and atheists as well. Again, this requirement would be acceptable to consequentialists and nonconsequentialists because as this minimal component of the Pauline Principle has been formulated there are no good consequentialist or nonconsequentialist reasons for violating it.[29] Theists and atheists should also accept this requirement as it applies to God for the same reasons that consequentialist and nonconsequentialists accept it. In virtue of this moral requirement, God should have acted so as to respect the moral preferences of those who would now have rights to such second-order goods, and that would have eliminated the need for those goods. But clearly this has not been done.

Goods to Which We Do Not Have a Right

With respect to goods to which we do not have a right, not providing such goods, even when we could easily do so, is not morally evil. Such goods are also either first-order goods that do not logically depend on serious wrongdoing or second-order goods that do logically depend on the existence of serious wrongdoing. For all such goods, the basic moral requirement that governs God's provision of them is:

Moral Evil Prevention Requirement III

Do not permit, rather than prevent, significant and especially horrendous evil consequences of immoral actions (which would violate someone's rights) in order to provide such goods when there are countless morally unobjectionable ways of providing those goods.

This requirement too is an exceptionless minimal component of the Pauline Principle which would be acceptable to consequentialists and nonconsequentialists as well as theists and atheists alike. Again, this requirement would be acceptable to consequentialists and nonconsequentialists because as this minimal component of the Pauline Principle has been formulated there are no good consequentialist or nonconsequentialist reasons for violating it.[30] However, theists also believe that God, without violating this requirement, can be justified in permitting significant and especially horrendous evil consequences of immoral action in order to provide goods to which we do not have a right.[31] Atheists would just love to be able to demonstrate that theists are mistaken about this.

First-Order Goods to Which We Do Not Have a Right
With respect to first-order goods to which we do not have a right, then both God and ourselves would have numerous ways of providing people with such goods without violating their rights by permitting rather than preventing significant and especially horrendous evil consequences of immoral actions to be inflicted on them. In cases, where we humans are causally constrained by the lack of resources and are thus unable to provide someone with such a good without permitting the serious violation of the person's rights, God would never be subject to such causal constraints, and it would be contradictory to assume that he is subject to logical constraints here.[32]

Second-Order Goods to Which We Do Not Have a Right
Unlike first-order goods to which we do not have a right, the very possibility of second-order goods to which we do not have a right is conditional on the existence of moral wrongdoing. For example, consider the opportunity to console a rape victim. No one is entitled to be provided with such a good and its very existence depends upon God's permission of a rape. Given then that the would-be beneficiaries of this good would morally prefer that God had prevented the rape rather than that they receive this good, God should have acted to respect their moral preferences. Even the perpetrators of such wrongful deeds, who later have the opportunity to repent them and seek forgiveness, would always morally

prefer that God had prevented the external consequences of their immoral deeds. So in virtue of Moral Evil Prevention Requirement II, God should have acted to respect the moral preferences of all those who are the beneficiaries of second-order goods to which they do not have a right and not have permitted significant and especially horrendous evil consequences of immoral actions on which such goods depend for their existence.

In sum, all goods that could be provided to us are either goods to which we have a right or goods to which we do not have a right. Each of these types further divides into first-order goods that do not logically depend on moral wrongdoing and second-order goods that do logically depend on moral wrongdoing. Given in virtue of Moral Evil Prevention Requirement II, that God is morally required to eliminate the need for second-order goods of either type, there is no need to further consider such goods here. With respect to first-order goods, the Moral Evil Prevention Requirements I and III morally constrain the pursuit of greater good justifications for both God and ourselves.

X

Now it might be objected that if God interfered with wrongdoing by preventing rather than permitting their significant or even horrendous evil consequences, God would be limiting the wrongdoer's freedom. This is true, but in each and every case where God would thus be limiting a wrongdoer's freedom by preventing rather than permitting significant and especially horrendous evil consequences of his wrongful action, God would also be securing a more important freedom for the would-be victim. So in terms of freedom, it would be better for God to prevent significant or even horrendous consequences of wrongdoing thereby restricting the wrongdoer's freedom than to permit significant or even horrendous consequences of wrongdoing, thereby restricting the freedom of the victim. So any justification in terms of freedom alone (contrary to the Free-Will Defense) would favor the freedom of the would-be victims over the freedom of the would-be perpetrators of wrongdoing.[33]

It might also be objected that while it may seem appropriate, even required, for God not to prevent, rather than to permit, significant and especially horrendous evil consequences of immoral actions in any particular case, once we generalize that behavior for all such cases, morally objectionable consequences result. Let us consider whether this is the case first with respect to first-goods to which we have a right and then with respect to first-goods to which we do not have a right.[34]

Thus, suppose, using a different example from those used previously, you are a West African living just as the slave trade is about to begin.[35] Suppose a Portuguese ship has arrived off the West African coast and you know its crew intends to trick members of a neighboring tribe to board the ship where they will then be subdued and taken off to be sold as slaves. Suppose that you are doing your best to warn them but you manage to warn only some but not all of those who intend to board the ship of the fate that awaits them. Suppose that God were then to intervene with a totally unexpected storm that prevents the ship from sailing away with its captives. Presumably, you would be happy with God's intervention in such a case.

Now imagine you are again considering whether to intervene to prevent the crew of another Portuguese ship from tricking members of still another tribe to board its ship. You might reason that if you did intervene you might well be completely successful this time. Yet upon further reflection you might decide that there is really no need for you to intervene because if you do nothing, you now assume that God would again intervene as he had done before and prevent the significantly evil consequences in this case. So you do nothing.

According to some theists, this is just the sort of behavior we would expect if God were to regularly intervene to prevent the evil consequences of our actions. Hence, they claim, this explains why God does not normally intervene to prevent the significant evil consequences of our wrongful actions. If God did normally intervene, on their account, we would lose the motivation we have to intervene ourselves, and thereby fail to utilize the opportunities we have for soul-making. Interestingly, some atheists also think that we would no longer be motivated to intervene ourselves if God did normally intervene to prevent the evil consequences of our wrongful actions. They just claim that is what God should do. A good God, they maintain, would always prevent evil consequences of wrongful actions, irrespective of whether such interventions eliminate possibilities for soul-making.

Now I want to reject both of these views and maintain that there is a third option, one that would be morally required for God which involves limited intervention. To see how this would work, consider again the second case where you decided not to intervene to prevent significantly evil consequences to the members of another West African tribe on the assumption that God would prevent those consequences in a similar way to the way he had before when you tried your best but were unsuccessful in warning all those who were in danger. Suppose what happens next is not exactly what you had expected. Yes, God does intervene to prevent the evil consequences, but that intervention is only partially successful. Originally, let's say, on this second occasion, you were in a position to warn all the West Africans that the Portuguese crew was intending to abduct them. Now that you have chosen to do nothing, you witness the Portuguese successfully sailing away with its captive West Africans. It is only a few hours later that you again see this same Portuguese ship this time accompanied by a French man of war (the French in this account are vehemently opposed to slavery). You see that the Portuguese crew are forced to disembark its captives who you observe are a bit traumatized, but otherwise unharmed. So you assume, not unreasonably, that God was involved in this intervention as well as in the earlier one. Nevertheless, you cannot help but note that this intervention was not as completely successful as it presumably would have been if you had chosen to intervene yourself. After all, you were in a position this time to keep all the West Africans from even boarding the Portuguese ship. As a result, the West Africans would not have been traumatized at all as they were during the short time they were captives of the Portuguese.

So you begin to detect a pattern. When you choose to intervene to prevent significantly evil consequences of wrongdoers, you will either be completely successful or your intervention will fall short. When the latter is going to happen, God does something to make the intervention completely successful. Likewise, when you choose not to intervene to prevent significant evil consequences, God again intervenes but this time not in a fully successful way. In cases of this sort, there is a residue of evil consequences that the victims still do suffer. This residue is not really a significant evil in its own right, but it is harmful nonetheless, and it is something for which you are primarily responsible. You could have prevented those harmful consequences but you chose not to do so and that makes you responsible for them. Of course, God too could have prevented those harmful consequences from happening even if you had decided not to do what you could to prevent them yourself. It is just that in such cases God would have chosen not to fully intervene and completely prevent all the evil consequences in order to leave you with a constrained opportunity for soul-making. Moreover, I maintain that this is exactly what God would be morally required to do.

Yet wouldn't such a policy of limited intervention by God constrain good people from being supervirtuous at the same time that it constrains bad people from being the supervicious? If God is going to consistently prevent the significantly evil consequences of our actions, then both good people and bad people are going to be restricted from inflicting significantly evil consequences on others. That means that good people will not be able to be as virtuous as they could otherwise be if they freely could have refrained from inflicting significantly evil consequences on others. It also means that bad people will not be able to be as vicious as they could otherwise be if they could freely inflict significantly evil consequences on others. But is this a problem? Who would object to God's following such a policy? Of course, bad people might object because such a policy limits them in the exercise of their superviciousness. But there is no reason why God or anyone else should listen to their objection in this regard. What about good people? Would they object to such a policy? How could they? True, the policy does limit good people in the exercise of their supervirtuousness, but that is just what it takes to consistently protect would-be victims from significant and especially horrendous evil consequences of the actions of bad people. Surely, good people would find the prevention of the infliction of such consequences on would-be victims by the supervicious worth the constraint imposed on how supervirtuous they themselves could be. In fact, they should find such tradeoffs not only morally acceptable but also morally required.

Nor would good people ever want to wish away the backup role God would have with regard to their attempts to prevent significant and especially the horrendous consequences of immoral actions. Good people would see this as the only way to guarantee that significant and especially the horrendous consequences of immoral actions will not be inflicted on their would-be victims. They would also welcome their first-responder role in the prevention of evil consequences of immoral actions recognizing that their failure to embrace that role would also render them responsible for at least some of the evil that would be inflicted on innocent victims—something good people surely would not want that to be the case.

XI

In the foregoing example, we have been dealing simply with first-order goods to which people have a right. Since we have a right to those goods, others are in a position to provide them to us. Almost the opposite is true of first-order goods to which we do not have a right. Only for some of those goods are others in a position to provide to them to us while for other such goods only God would be in a position to provide them to us.

Call the first sort of goods human-option goods and the second sort divine-only-option goods. Now only with respect to human-option goods could God and ourselves be competing to provide them. So only with respect to such goods should God, for reasons of soul-making, be following the limited interventionist policy that I have been advocating for such contexts. By contrast, with respect to divine-only-option goods, which humans cannot ever provide, there are no grounds for limiting God's intervention to secure such goods to which we have a right except Moral Evil Prevention Requirement III.

XII

In sum, this chapter has examined Brian Davies's attempt to use the work of Thomas Aquinas to defend traditional theism by dropping the assumption that God is a moral agent who needs to act in a morally justified manner. Here are its conclusions:

1. Davies's claim that the moral language of virtue and obligation does not apply to God is more stipulated than argued for.

2. Davies's view cannot be supported by a pure divine command theory.
3. As part of Davies's own rejection of divine command theory, he argues that God cannot command us to do anything that goes against the law of reason that God has embedded in our hearts because that would involve God in a contradiction. Granting this, I argued that God also could not act against that same law of reason that he embedded in our hearts which applies to all rational agents including God himself because that too would involve God in a contradiction.
4. Even assuming that God were not subject to moral requirements as Davies contends, God's failure, if he existed, to prevent the horrendous evil consequences of all the immoral actions in the world when he could easily have done so without either producing a greater evil or failing to secure a greater good is still to be condemned. It would have resulted in far more evil consequences than has been produced individually by all the greatest villains among us.
5. Davies's attempt to characterize God as good in some other way that does not involve being morally good was found wanting.
6. Davies's attempt to get closer to the conclusion he wants by showing that God is not causally connected in any problematic way to evil was shown not to work because it similarly would hold of human wrongdoers.
7. A different attempt by Aquinas to defend God by distancing him from moral evil, but not natural evil, was also found to be unsuccessful.
8. Finally, the question as to whether any moral justification for God's permission of significant and particularly horrendous evil consequences of immoral actions could be provided was directly addressed. Here, drawing together parts of the arguments of previous chapters and developing them further, a relatively free-standing argument was provided showing that God's permission of significant and especially horrendous evil consequences of immoral action is logically incompatible with morally exceptionless minimal components of the Pauline Principle, that is, with components of the Pauline Principle that no defensible moral theory can reject.

Notes

1. I will use "Davies" for "Davies interpreting Aquinas" unless otherwise indicated.
2. See Davies (2006, p. 224). See also Davies (2011, p. 63). But even here there must be some sound basis for the metaphorical language. God must be treating us in some way that is like the way that parents should treat their children.
3. Still, metaphorical statements do purport to be true and informative. Think of our use of metaphor/simile in physics. We say the atom is like our solar system, claiming that its nucleus is like the sun and its electrons are like the planets orbiting around the sun.
4. There are impure or modified forms of divine command which find the standard of morality in God's nature such that even God could not go against that standard. One such theory, defended by Robert Adams, maintains that what is right is determined by the commands of a loving God. See Adams (1979, pp. 66–79). But the important question to ask here is whether God's commands are to be understood not to conflict with the morality that God presumably imbedded in human nature. Only pure divine command theory would maintain that they would so conflict. So from now on I will use "divine command theory" to refer to "pure divine command theory."
5. The problem of evil also cannot even get started on a subjectivist account of morality. This raises the question of what John Mackie, who was a moral subjectivist, thought he was doing when using the problem of evil to challenge the existence of God. See Mackie (1982). The answer seems to be that he saw himself as just arguing from the objectivist account of morality that theists accept.
6. See, for example, Ockham (1979).
7. Nor should he because as I have argued on pure divine theory the problem of evil is simply denied. Plantinga in his debate with Mackie knew he could not use this approach to solve the problem of evil.
8. God could, of course, change our nature so that what was good for us would correspondingly change. For example, God could make us such that if you put a knife into my chest, I would immediately die and then spring back to life again with tremendous pleasure. Then the law of nature for us would be different, and God's commands and action

toward us would presumably change to reflect this difference in our nature.

9. It might be objected that natural law only applies to beings in virtue of their belonging to a certain kind or kinds and God does not belong to any kind of being, and so natural law does not apply to him. Nevertheless, God is said to be rational and it is in virtue of his being rational that the same (moral) natural law applies to God as to ourselves.

10. If God could easily prevent horrendous consequences of our wrongful actions without causing greater harm or failing to achieve a greater good, it could not simply be a matter of supererogation whether or not he does so. That would not be the case for us and it should not be the case for God.

11. This is because God, if he exists, would have to be permitting all the significant and especially the horrendous consequences of immoral action of all the great villains in the world in addition to all other such consequences that occur in the world.

12. For example, no scientist today thinks that rocks seek their own good.

13. Here too we have to allow for exceptions. We, for example, are not seeking our own good when we act out of whim or act neurotically.

14. This is a very troubling aspect of Davies's view. In *The Reality of God and the Problem of Evil* and *Thomas Aquinas on God and Evil,* Davies repeatedly claims that in effect God cannot be held responsible for the evil in the world because he does not will evil as an end itself. But I argued in the text that it shows nothing of the sort since the same holds true of the worst of moral criminals throughout human history.

15. The wolf ultimately would die by starvation and the deer would die more immediately and more violently. However, as species, the wolf and the deer can flourish together, with wolves pruning deer of their weakest members and deer pruning wolves of their most ineffective hunters. Yet as individuals, when they come into serious conflict, they are engaged in a deadly zero-sum game.

16. There is no other possibility except that we could act in both ways with respect to different consequences of our action.

17. Again, it is worth noting that the course of argument we are pursuing here is available only to a deontologist who thinks that there could be exceptions to the requirement never to do or permit evil that good may come of it or that sometimes the end will justify the means. An absolute deontologist would summarily reject this line of argument and therefore

would immediately be led to the conclusion that God does not exist. Here I am assuming that the absolute deontologist is mistaken about this. Later, however, I will base my argument on specific moral requirements that are acceptable to both consequentialist and deontologists alike, including absolute deontologists.

18. See Aquinas (1947, 1A 2.3 Ad. 1). We also have scriptural support for the view, "God works in all things for the good" (Romans 8:28).

19. See, for example, Wykstra (1984, pp. 75–77) and Penelhum (1966–67, p. 107).

20. First put forward by Thompson (1985, pp. 1395–1415).

21. Now one might interpret preserving the life of the innocent would-be victim in this case as the "greater good," but this would render the standard tautological. It would be preferable to say that pursuing the greater good is not morally justified in this case, or that in this case pursuing what would otherwise be a greater moral good is not morally justified. However, God, given the unlimited options available to him, could always meet such constraints without sacrificing any greater good.

22. See the previous endnote.

23. This will imply that someone who can easily make such a provision will have an obligation to provide the relevant goods.

24. Again, this will imply that someone who can easily make such a provision will have an obligation to provide the relevant goods.

25. As it should be, these moral requirements apply to us as well as to God, although our ability to prevent is obviously different.

26. Note that consequentialists can accept the constraint of this minimal component of the Pauline Principle because it has a consequentialist as well as a nonconsequentialist justification.

27. This is because they think that it may be logically impossible for God to prevent the evil consequences of both such actions.

28. See the argument for this in the previous chapter.

29. Consequentialists and nonconsequentialists would both accept this requirement at least as it applies to God for whom there would always be viable analogous goods he could provide that would not require permitting significant and especially horrendous evil consequences of immoral actions. See, for example, to discussion of Matthew Shepard in Chap. 2. Moreover, to claim that it may be logically impossible for God to provide analogous goods without permitting significant and especially horrendous evil consequences of immoral actions would make God impossibly less powerful than ourselves.

30. Again, note that consequentialists can accept the constraint of this minimal component of the Pauline Principle because it has a consequentialist as well as a nonconsequentialist justification.
31. This is because theists think that there may be no logically possible alternative way for God to provide for such goods that is morally unobjectionable.
32. See the argument for this in the previous chapter.
33. For further argument, see Chap. 2.
34. Given the previous argument that God should eliminate the need for second-order goods of either type, there is no need to consider such goods here.
35. Here the example focuses on global justice.

Bibliography

Adams, Robert Merrihew. 1979. Divine Command Metaethics Modified Again. *Journal of Religious Studies* 7: 66–79.

Aquinas, Thomas 1947. *Summa Theologiae*. Trans. The Fathers of the English Dominican Province. New York: Benziger Brother Inc.

Davies, Brian. 2006. *The Reality of God and the Problem of Evil*. London/New York: Continuum.

———. 2009. Is God a Moral Agent? In *Whose God? Which Tradition?* ed. D.Z. Phillips. Hampshire: Ashgate.

———. 2011. *Thomas Aquinas on Good and Evil*. Oxford: Oxford University Press.

Mackie, J.L. 1982. *The Miracle of Theism*. Oxford: Oxford University Press.

Penelhum, Terence. 1966–67. Divine Goodness and the Problem of Evil. *Religious Studies* 2: 95–107.

Rowe, William. 1979. The Problem of Evil and some Varieties of Atheism. *American Philosophical Quarterly* 16: 335–341.

Thompson, Judith Jarvis. 1985. The Trolley Problem. *Yale Law Journal* 94: 1395–1415.

William of Ockham. 1979. On the Four Books of Sentences. In *Divine Command Morality*, ed. Janice Idziak. New York: Edwin Mellon Press.

Wykstra, Stephen. 1984. The Humean Obstacle to Evidential Arguments from Suffering. *International Journal for the Philosophy of Religion* 16 (2): 73–93.

7

What About a Redemptive God?

It might be objected to my logical argument against the existence of God that there is a justification for God's involvement with the evil in the world to be found in the long biblical history of God's seeking to bring redemption to a wayward humanity. There are two accounts of this salvation history: a Jewish one and a Christian one. Each offers a justification for God's involvement with the evil in the world. The Jewish account departs from the Christian one by not recognizing Jesus as the awaited for Messiah. The Christian one attempts to incorporate much of the Jewish one with the important difference that Jesus is taken to be the Christ, the Messiah. In each account, God is viewed as seeking to bring redemption to a wayward humanity. Both accounts share the same history of redemption until the coming of Jesus. That history, as one would expect, begins with the Book of Genesis.[1]

I

Following Adam and Eve's wrongdoing in the Garden of Eden, God is said to promise an appropriate response to the introduction of evil into the world (Genesis 3:15).[2] God's concern is further expressed in his

© The Author(s) 2019
J. P. Sterba, *Is a Good God Logically Possible?*,
https://doi.org/10.1007/978-3-030-05469-4_7

promise to Noah following the flood (Genesis 8:15–23). Then there is God's calling of Abraham and his promise to him after Abraham showed his willingness to sacrifice, Isaac, his only son (Genesis 22:15–19). God's promise to Abraham is reaffirmed to Isaac, then to Jacob, his son, renamed Israel, and later to Israel's entire extended family when they journey to Egypt in order to avoid famine in the land of Canaan (Genesis 24–46).

After initially faring well and multiplying in the land of Egypt, the descendants of Israel are enslaved when a new Pharaoh comes to power. Here again, God is said to intervene and raise up Moses as a leader to free the Israelites from the land of Egypt. (Exodus 1–4) There follows a dramatic struggle between Moses and the Pharaoh requiring ten plagues and the parting of a sea before the Israelites are actually able to leave Egypt (Exodus 5–15).

On their way to the promised land, the Israelites show themselves unfaithful to the covenant they have with God. So they are required to wander for forty years in the desert. Only then under the new leadership of Joshua are they permitted to enter the promised land. Yet once they are there, the Israelites are still not able to fully take control of the land from the local inhabitants (Joshua 1–12).

During this period, natural leaders called Judges arise from time to time inspiring the Israelites to recommit themselves to their covenant with God which enables them under the leadership of one particular judge or another to triumph as least temporarily over their enemies (Judges 1–17).

After many years of being led by various judges, the prophet Samuel, having consulted with God, appointed Saul king over Israel (I Kings 8–10). Saul was initially successful against Israel's enemies and was said to find favor with God, but when Saul failed to follow God's command to kill Amalek and destroy all of his cattle, he was said to be no longer in God's favor (I Kings 11–15). Shortly thereafter, God commands Samuel to anoint a young shepherd, named David, king of Israel, even though Saul continued to rule until he and his sons were killed by the Philistines (I Kings 16–31).

After building his own royal palace, David wanted to build a temple for God in Jerusalem to replace the tent in which the Ark of the Covenant was kept. But through the prophet Nathan, God told David that it would be Solomon, his son, who would build the temple. After David's death, Solomon enjoys a glorious reign, and he does indeed build a temple to God (II Kings, 1–24, III Kings 1–11).

Israel is split into two monarchies following the death of Solomon. His son Rehoboam ruled in Jerusalem over the tribes of Judah and Benjamin, while Jeroboam of the tribe of Ephraim ruled the other ten tribes. After some time, the ten tribes of the northern kingdom are sent into exile by the Assyrians and eventually they lose contact with the kingdom of Judah (III Kings 12–17).

The kingdom of Judah too comes to an end when Nebuchadnezzar, king of Babylon, invades Judah and exiles its elite and subsequently destroys its temple (III Kings 18–25). About fifty years later, a group of Jews return to resettle in Judah and one of their leaders Zerubbabel of the house of David oversees the construction of a new temple (I Esdras 1–6).

At this time, the Jews were often ruled by foreign kings and their proxies until 139 BCE when the Hasmonean family of Aaronic priestly stock seizes the throne (I Maccabees 1–16). In 36 BCE, however, Herod, an Edomite, kills the Hasmonean King Antigonus and takes the throne for himself as a Roman client king. Herod renovates the temple in Jerusalem, creating an edifice so magnificent that it was said, "He who has not seen Herod's temple has never seen a beautiful building in all his days." Upon Herod's death, the Romans divide his kingdom among three of his sons and his sister.[3]

In 66 CE, the Jews living in Judea revolt against their Roman overlords. By 68 CE, the Romans had eradicated resistance in Northern Judea and they turned their attention to the subjugation of Jerusalem. They breach the city's outer walls in 70 CE, loot the city, and destroy the temple. Thousands are slaughtered while thousands of those who are spared are enslaved and sent throughout the Roman Empire. The temple in Jerusalem is never rebuilt (Josephus 1984).

II

About thirty-five years before the destruction of the temple in Jerusalem, Jesus of Nazareth began preaching that the Kingdom of God is at hand and that only through him can anyone enter it. After preaching and working miracles for a relatively brief period of time, he journeys to

Jerusalem, where the Romans crucify him at the behest of the Jewish leadership (Montefiore 1927).

The teachings and miracles of Jesus and especially his proclaimed resurrection from the dead are taken by his disciples to demonstrate that he is the Messiah that the Jews have long been awaiting. While many Jews were looking for the Messiah to establish God's kingdom in this world, Jesus proclaimed that his kingdom was not of this world (Ibid.).

Jesus is viewed by his disciples as the fulfillment of the promises made by God throughout the Old Testament.[4] According to St. Paul, just as death and destruction entered the world with the wrongdoing of the first Adam and the subsequent wrongdoing of those who came after him, so too, through Jesus Christ, the second Adam, God has made redemption available to all. While God could have left us to just suffer from the effects of human wrongdoing, he instead chose to send his son to enable us to restore our relationship with the Godhead (Romans 5:12, I Corinthians 15:45). As John put it in his gospel, "God so loved the world that he gave his one and only Son, that whoever believes in him shall not perish but have eternal life" (John 3:16).

According to one interpretation of the Christian view, God was offended by the wrongdoing of Adam and Eve as well as the wrongdoing of the rest of us who came after them. Moreover, assuming that offenses are measured by whom they are offenses against, that made our offenses against God infinitely bad. So while divine justice demands satisfaction for those offenses, we, finite creatures that we are, are incapable of providing the infinite satisfaction required by our offenses. Truly adequate satisfaction could then be made only by someone who is divine, and thus capable of providing infinite satisfaction. Moreover, atonement for humanity could be made only by someone who is also fully human as well as fully divine, which, of course, is just what Jesus was proclaimed to be. Thus by freely taking it upon himself to offer his own life on our behalf, Jesus, through his passion and death, accrues infinite merit, thereby providing fully adequate satisfaction for all our wrongdoing. While the infinite merit of any one of Jesus's actions was sufficient to earn the redemption of all of us, it was fitting that the meritorious value of all of Christ's actions should culminate in his passion and death (Hogan 1963, p. 39). As the Council of Trent put it, "By his most holy passion on the wood of the cross, Christ made satisfaction for us to God the Father."[5]

Now this is just one Christian account of how redemption occurs. It is found in the New Testament as my references indicate. It is also developed more fully in St. Anselm.[6] It is frequently referred to as the satisfaction account because it attempts to explain how satisfaction is provided to God for our sins. There is also another account with some New Testament support that was developed earlier by Origen of Alexandria according to which Jesus is said to ransom us from the Devil. This is frequently referred to as the ransom account.[7] Still another is the moral influence account developed during the Enlightenment that sees Christ through his death and resurrection leading us to moral change (Wallace and Rusk 2011). As I see it, all such accounts of redemption suffer from the same defect.[8]

III

So I will focus on the Christian account and show how it fails to justify God's involvement with significant and especially horrendous evil in the world before turning to the Jewish account. I will then indicate how the standard Jewish account fails for the very same reason as the Christian account. Neither account, I argue, can provide a justification for what would have to be God's involvement with significant and especially horrendous moral evil in our world.

Redemption is, of course, required because of human wrongdoing, and initially two types of wrongdoing appear to be at stake here. The first is wrongdoing that is directed against God. The second is wrongdoing that is directed against other living beings. Now most discussions of the need for redemption focus on wrongdoing directed against God. Frequently, this wrongdoing is described as disobedience to God's commands. Sometimes, it is also characterized as a refusal of God's love, or a rejection of God's offer of friendship (Wiley 2002).

Unfortunately, there is a fundamental difficulty with conceiving of wrongdoing in this way. The difficulty is that once we conceive of God in the traditional sense as an omni-God who is all good and all powerful, it follows that nothing we can ever do could harm such a God. Putting this together with a standard principle in legal ethics that wrongdoing of the seriously punishable kind always presupposes the infliction or risk of harm, it follows that we cannot wrong God, certainly we cannot do anything against God that would make it appropriate for anyone to suffer and die for what we have done in that regard.[9]

Of course, it could be argued that when we harm God's creatures we harm God just the way that when we normally harm someone's child we normally harm the parents of the child as well. Yet if God is truly perfect he cannot be made vulnerable by creating in the way that we can be made vulnerable by procreating. So God, if he is truly perfect, cannot be harmed in this way, although we can.

Nor would it do to claim that since God loves us and desires that we love him, he can be harmed by those who do not return his love. This is because what God presumably wants for us is that we have the choice to love him freely or not. Assuming then that we have this choice and exercise it either in this life or in some afterlife, God will have achieved just what he wants, and so he would not have been harmed by our choice however we make it.

Now St. Anselm once argued that since God is an infinite being, all of our wrongdoing against God has infinite disvalue creating a debt that requires something of comparable positive value if it is to be repaid (Anselm 2007). But if our wrongdoing against God actually causes no harm at all, then such harmless acts could not be the source of infinite disvalue to God.

Suppose then we grant that we cannot account for our need for redemption in this way, why then couldn't we ground it simply on the harm we do to other human beings, or even the harm we do to nonhuman creatures? This clearly seems to be a promising option.[10]

Indeed, the harm we do to our fellow creatures is severe enough to constitute serious wrongdoing, as our legal ethics attests. And while such harm would not be harm directed against God, God could still take such harm into account, and seek to appropriately limit it, as needed, and help redeem those who inflict it, as needed. In this, God would be acting in the way we would expect an ideally just and powerful political state to act.

For such a state, redemption of wrongdoers would clearly be an important task. But it would not be as important as the task of preventing the inflicting of significant and especially horrendous harmful consequences of immoral actions on their would-be victims in the first place. For such a state, taking appropriate measures to limit the infliction of such consequences on would-be victims (in accord with Moral Evil Prevention Requirements I, II, and III) would have both temporal and moral priority over any measures to redeem wrongdoers.[11]

Nor would an ideally just and powerful political state try to prevent all the immoral consequences that occur in its domain, even if that were within its power to do so. Instead, it would focus on preventing significant and especially horrendous immoral consequences that impact people's lives. It would not seek to prevent lesser consequences because any general attempt to do so would tend to interfere with people's significant freedoms.[12] Rather, a just state would leave such evils to be used by individuals for soul-making as far as possible. Only then, after completing this prior task of prevention, would an ideally just and powerful state take up the task of redeeming wrongdoers.

Similarly, God, like a just political state, should not try to prevent every moral evil. Instead, like a just political state, God should focus on preventing significant and especially horrendous immoral consequences that impact people's lives, as needed (in accord with Moral Evil Prevention Requirements I, II, and III).[13] God should not seek to prevent lesser consequences because any general attempt to do so would tend to interfere with people's significant freedoms. Accordingly, God, like the just political state, should leave such evils to be used by individuals for soul-making as far as possible. Only then, after completing this first task of prevention, should God take up the task of the redemption of wrongdoers.

Moreover, at least for morally horrendously evil consequences, Moral Evil Prevention Requirements I, II, and III apply first to political states, and only when those states either cannot, or wrongfully do not, meet them, do they apply to individuals, particularly, but not exclusively, to the individuals who are responsible for the actions of those states, and only when such individuals either cannot or wrongfully will not meet the requirements do they then apply to God. What this order of application ensures is that as much soul-making obtains as is consistent with the meeting of these exceptionless minimal moral requirements. Of course, if God exists, it is possible that in virtue of our interactions with him, still other moral requirements could arise for us. It is just that these additional moral requirements could never override the application of Moral Evil Prevention Requirements I, II, and III first to a political state, then to ourselves, and finally to God.

IV

Now it is sometimes claimed that God had a choice as to whether to redeem us or not, that it was morally open for him to go either way.[14] But this can't be right. Everyone, including God, should be open to restoring relations to an appropriate degree when they have become morally disrupted by wrongdoing. While we might allow that God was (morally) free to create or not, once God chooses to create then obligations to any and all creatures that have a good of their own arise for God just the way obligations arise for us when we choose to bring children into the world by procreation.

Nor would it be morally acceptable for God just to engage in redemption of wrongdoing while ignoring the more important task of prevention, specifically the task of preventing significant and especially horrendous harmful consequences of immoral actions from being inflicted on their would-be victims, when that can easily be done without either producing more harmful results or forgoing more beneficial results. Hence, a God who always permits significant, and especially horrendous, harmful consequences of immoral actions when he could easily have prevented them without either producing more harmful results or forgoing more beneficial results could not be called good by any stretch of our imagination.[15]

Given then that the task of preventing significant and especially horrendous harmful consequences of immoral actions would always have priority over the task of redeeming wrongdoing in an ideally just and powerful political state, the need for redemption is going to be thereby reduced. Yet who would complain about this prioritizing of prevention? Surely not the would-be victims who would otherwise have significant and especially horrendous harmful consequences inflicted on them; nor those who would otherwise minister to those who would be victims because they would prefer to become virtuous in some other way; nor those who later would repent their wrongdoing and wish that God had prevented at least the harmful consequences of their actions. Clearly, only those who are unwaveringly committed to significant and especially horrendous wrongdoing would complain about God's acting in this way. Yet no one else should be moved by such complaints.

Now consider whether in a world where God would give priority to the prevention of wrongful harm over the redemption of wrongdoers, there still would be any need for God to become incarnate for the sake of wrongdoers. Recall that in the Christian view, there is no necessity that God become incarnate and suffer and die in order to redeem us. Even in our world, God could always have redeemed us without becoming incarnate and dying on a cross. In the Christian view, God's becoming incarnate, and suffering and dying on a cross, is just an appropriate way for God to help accomplish our redemption (Hogan 1963, pp. 16–17, 39). So in a world where God gave priority to the prevention of wrongful harm over the redemption of wrongdoers, God could still become incarnate to help redeem us, subject to at least two important constraints.

First, such a redeemer would only be concerned with redeeming our harmful wrongdoings or just intended harmful wrongdoings against fellow creatures. Given that it is impossible for us to harm God, the only wrongdoing that needs redemption would have to be our harmful wrongdoings or just intended harmful wrongdoings against our fellow creatures.[16]

Secondly, in a world where God would give priority to the prevention of significant and especially horrendous harmful consequences of immoral action, any redeemer would not suffer an ignominious death on a cross. God, just like an ideally just and powerful political state, would always prevent such consequence. Thus, any redeemer would be more like a Nelson Mandela, a Dolores Huerta, or a Mohandas Gandhi (without his assassination), each of whom in different ways opened up a path of redemption for wrongdoers in their societies. Still, such a redeemer would be different from these moral leaders in our world because he would be proclaiming a path of redemption in a context where God had already contained wrongdoing by preventing significant and especially horrendous evil consequences of immoral actions.

Sometimes, it is argued that what is attractive about Jesus from a Christian perspective is that he suffered along with us, experiencing some of the worse consequences of the immoral actions that anyone can encounter in our world. Yet what would be so attractive about someone suffering along with us if that person could easily have prevented both his and our suffering without either producing more harmful results or forgoing more beneficial results? With such benefactors who needs enemies?

Of course, there is nothing wrong with people seeking redemption for themselves and others with respect to their past wrongdoing. Clearly, we should be pleased to see people attempting to redeem themselves and others in this way. We can even understand the attraction wrongdoers find in their wrongful behavior that typically benefits themselves at the expense of others. We can only hope that once they have been reformed, they will remain committed to acting in a way that fairly takes into account everyone's welfare.[17]

Yet what if we were told of someone who is behaving very badly thereby harming many that he could easily have avoided harming also happens to wants to redeem others who are engaged in wrongdoing. What would we think of such a redeemer? Wouldn't we find a contradiction imbedded in his behavior? Wouldn't we conclude that no one could consistently be engaged in the moral task of redeeming of others while permitting significant and especially horrendous harmful consequences of immoral actions to be inflicted on them that he could easily have prevented without either producing more harmful results or forgoing more beneficial results? So while we can imagine how someone, like ourselves, might be caught up in such inconsistent behavior, clearly we could not attribute such behavior to an all-good, all-powerful God. Hence, God, if he existed, would give temporal and moral priority to the prevention of significant and especially the horrendous evil consequences of immoral action when he could easily do so without producing more harmful results or forgoing more beneficial results. This God would do prior to taking up the task of redeeming wrongdoers. Of course, nothing like the widespread prevention of significant and especially horrendous evil consequences of immoral action obtains in our world, and that is logically incompatible with God's existence.

So this Christian account of salvation history has a contradiction embedded in it. It portrays a God who has long sought our redemption while being forced to admit that that same God is not engaged in the prevention of significant and especially the horrendous evil consequences of immoral action. Thus, while the existence of God is certainly compatible with a long history of God's seeking our redemption, it is not logically compatible with an equally long history of what would have to be God's failing to prevent significant and especially the horrendous evil consequences of immoral action when he could easily do so without producing more harmful results or forgoing more beneficial results.[18]

Now the standard Jewish account of salvation history faces the same problem.[19] It too has a contradiction embedded in it. While the Jewish account proclaims a long history of God's seeking our redemption, without recognizing Jesus as the Messiah, it too is forced to admit that God is not engaged in the prevention of significant and especially the horrendous evil consequences of immoral action. Accordingly, while the existence of God is certainly compatible with a long history of God's seeking our redemption found in the Jewish account, it is not logically compatible with an equally long history of God's failing to prevent significant and especially the horrendous evil consequences of immoral action when he could easily have done so without producing more harmful results or forgoing more beneficial results.

V

So neither Christian nor Jewish accounts of salvation history can overcome the logical argument against the existence of God developed in preceding chapters. That argument has rested on two sets of premises. One set are exceptionless minimal components of the Pauline Principle never to do evil that good may come of it. Those components are:

Moral Evil Prevention Requirement I
Prevent, rather than permit, significant and especially horrendous evil consequences of immoral actions without violating anyone's rights (a good to which we have a right) when that can easily be done.

Moral Evil Prevention Requirement II

Do not permit, rather than prevent, significant and especially horrendous evil consequences of immoral actions simply to provide other rational beings with goods they would morally prefer not to have.

Moral Evil Prevention Requirement III

Do not permit, rather than prevent, significant and especially horrendous evil consequences of immoral actions on would-be victims (which would violate their rights) in order to provide them with goods to which they do not have a right, when there are countless morally unobjectionable ways of providing those goods.[20]

The other set of premises are those imbedded in the analogy of an ideally just and powerful political state. That analogy is based on the ideal of a just political state, which assumes that states, like individuals, would be required to abide by Moral Evil Prevention Requirements I–III. A just political state, however, would typically have greater resources for abiding by these principles than individuals by themselves would have. The analogy of an ideally just and powerful political state simply further extends imaginatively what such a state would be capable of doing if its goodness and power approached the goodness and power that God is supposed to have. Since we know that such a state would be actively engaged in the prevention of significant and especially horrendous harmful consequences of immoral actions, we know that God, if he exists, would have to be doing the same.

Now there are three other premises to my argument that initially appear independent of the two I have just mentioned. One is that in our moral imaginations we expect superheroes to restrict the freedom of villains in order to prevent them from restricting the more important freedoms of would-be victims. Another is that there is a great loss of significant freedom in our world due to all the evil that is not prevented in it. These premises are developed in Chap. 2. The third premise is the claim that it is possible to integrate our having adequate opportunities to prevent evil ourselves with God's always being there to prevent significant and especially horrendous evil consequences of immoral actions as needed. This premise is argued for in Chaps. 4, 5, and 6.

As it turns out, the first two of these premises are actually built into the analogy of an ideally just and powerful state. This is because this analogy assumes that there would be a great loss of significant freedom in the world if either an ideally just and powerful state or God, in place of our imaginary superheroes, were not actively involved in preventing such a loss. So, in this way, the analogy of an ideally just and powerful state incorporates the freedom premise.

The third premise which is about its being possible to ideally integrate our having adequate opportunities to prevent evil ourselves with God's being there to prevent significant and especially horrendous evil consequences of immoral actions himself, as needed, is also built into the analogy of an ideally just and powerful state. This is because the analogy is designed to show that an ideally just and powerful state and its members can work together in a way that both would be virtuous in morally appropriate ways.

So my logical argument against the existence of God just rests primarily on (1) exceptionless minimal components of the Pauline Principle (Moral Evil Prevention Requirements I–III), and (2) the analogy of an ideally just and powerful state. But it rests on more besides. For example, there is the premise (defended in Chaps. 4 and 5) that all the goods that can be provided to us can be divided into goods to which we have a right and goods to which we do not have a right, and the premise (defended in Chap. 5) that to assume that God would be facing logical impossibilities with regard to preventing significant and especially horrendous consequences of immoral actions when we would be facing just causal impossibilities leads to a contradiction.[21] It is only when all these premises are used together that we get my logical argument against the existence of God based on the problem of evil.[22]

Notes

1. I am assuming for the sake of argument the truth of this account of salvation history in order to determine whether a contradiction can be derived therefrom. For attempts to evaluate the historicity of this account, see Thompson (2002), Carrier (2014), and Ehrman (2016).

2. The Quran says that after Adam sinned, God forgave him and provided advice. "Thus did Adam disobey his Lord, so he went astray. Then his Lord chose him, and turned to him with forgiveness, and gave him guidance" (Surat Ta-Ha: 121–122). The Quran also says that wrongdoing is not passed down from parents to children. "That no burdened person (with sins) shall bear the burden (sins) of another. And that man can have nothing but what he does (of good and bad). And that his deeds will be seen, then he will be recompensed with a full and the best [fair] recompense" (Surat an-Najm: 38–41). In Islam, we seem to start out sinless and then are judged by our actions once we reach the age of reason. So there seems to be no comparable need for redemption as in the Jewish and Christian accounts.
3. See History of the Jewish Monarchy http://www.chabad.org/library/article_cdo/aid/1935026/jewish/A-History-of-the-Jewish-Monarchy.htm accessed 10/7/2018.
4. Since "Christ" means the anointed one; that is, the Messiah, Jesus, is called Christ by his disciples.
5. See The Council of Trent (1848).
6. See Anselm (2007, pp. 237–32).
7. See McDonald (1985, pp. 141–2).
8. Even Eleanore Stump's new account of redemption or atonement, which differs from these general accounts in some respects while similar in others, shares the same defect that I found in these other general accounts. See Stump (2018).
9. I am using harm in a broader sense to include offense. For the limitation of wrongdoing to causing or threating harm in this boarder sense, see Feinberg (1987–1990).
10. It might be claimed that we need redemption for the harm we do to ourselves. Yet that would be a strange claim to make. Actions that simply harm the agent who performs them are not typically punished by the law. Once we become competent agents, we are thought to be free to harm ourselves if we want to do so, as people do by smoking, overeating, and so on. Sad though such behavior may be, it is not easy to see that behavior as calling for redemption. Self-improvement or reform seems more appropriate. We certainly do not usually penalize people for engaging in such behavior.
11. See Chap. 6, pp. 8/16-11/16.
12. I am understanding significant freedoms to be primarily those freedoms a just political state would want to protect since that would fairly secure each person's fundamental interests.

13. Again, see Chap. 6, pp. 8/16-11/16.
14. See, for example, Hogan (1963, pp. 16–18).
15. Suppose the U.S., having developed a secret weapon that temporarily paralyzes people, could have easily stopped the external significant and especially horrendous evil consequences of the Holocaust and maybe those of World War II as a whole without causing any greater harm or forgoing any greater benefit. Suppose, in this context, the U.S. decided not to use its secret weapon. What would we think about the moral character of the U.S. 1939–1945?
16. Again, it might be claimed that we need redemption for the harm we do to ourselves. Yet this is surely strange claim to make. Actions that simply harm the agent who performs them are not typically punished by the law. Once we become competent agents, we are thought to be free to harm ourselves if we want to do so, as people do by smoking, overeating, and so on. Sad though such behavior may be, it is not easy to see that behavior as calling for redemption. Self-improvement or reform seems more appropriate. Still, if one wants to regard this as personal redemption, I could recognize it as such.
17. Hopefully, these reformed wrongdoers appreciate the rational and moral argument for so acting. See Sterba (2014).
18. It should be obvious that this critique applies to all accounts of Christian redemption. For another related critique that seems to also apply to all such accounts see Pogin (forthcoming).
19. See Babylonian Talmud, Tractate Rosh HaShanah (11b) and Talmud Yerushalmi, Tractate Berachot (2c).
20. Now the requirement typically holds even when the last clause does not, but it is clearly exceptionless when the last clause does obtain, as it always does for God.
21. In addition, if we were to assume that it is logically impossible for God to prevent significant and especially horrendous evil consequences of immoral actions that occur throughout the course of human history, then God could not be permitting those consequences either because God could only permit what he could also prevent, and to deny that God would be permitting evil would contradict the fundamental doctrine of traditional theism that God permits moral evil.
22. It is also important to see that all these premises relating to moral evil can be seen to fold into the premises of the argument given in the conclusion that John Mackie should have used to win his debate with Alvin Plantinga.

Bibliography

Anselm. 2007. Cur Deus Homo. In *Anselm: Basic Writings*, ed. Thomas Williams, 237–232. Indianapolis: Hackett Publishing.

Carrier, Richard. 2014. *On the Historicity of Jesus*. Sheffield: Sheffield Phoenix Press.

Ehrman, B. 2016. *Jesus Before the Gospels*. New York: HarperCollins.

Feinberg, Joel. 1987–1990. *The Moral Limits of the Criminal Law*. New York: Oxford University Press.

History of the Jewish Monarchy. http://www.chabad.org/library/article_cdo/aid/1935026/jewish/A-History-of-the-Jewish-Monarchy.htm.   Accessed 10/7/2018.

Hogan, William. 1963. *Christ's Redemptive Sacrifice*. Englewood Cliffs: Prentice-Hall.

Josephus, Flavius. 1984. *The Jewish War*. New York: Penguin.

McDonald, H.D. 1985. *The Atonement of the Death of Christ*. Grand Rapids: Baker Book House.

Montefiore, C.D., ed. 1927. *The Synoptic Gospels*. London: Macmillan.

Pogin, Kathryn. forthcoming. Conceptualizing the Atonement.

Sterba, James P. 2014. *From Rationality to Equality*. Oxford: Oxford University Press.

Stump, Eleanore. 2018. *Atonement*. New York: Oxford University Press.

The Council of Trent, The Sixth Session. 1848. Trans. J. Waterworth. London: Dolman.

Thompson, Thomas. 2002. *The Historicity of the Patriarchal Naratives*. Harrisburg: Trinity Press.

Wallace, A.J., and R.D. Rusk. 2011. *Moral Transformation: The Original Christian Paradigm of Salvation*. Auckland: Bridgehead.

Wiley, Tatha. 2002. *Original Sin*. Mahwah: The Paulist Press.

8

Taking Natural Evil into Account

Consider the wide array of natural evils we face in the world. They include earthquakes, volcanic eruptions, diseases, hurricanes, tornadoes, fires, lightning strikes, and floods.[1] These evils harm some while benefiting others. For example, a volcanic eruption may destroy whole villages while benefiting future inhabitants by enriching the soil. Some natural evils will also significantly harm humans while benefiting nonhumans if only by providing food for scavengers. Yet the same holds true for the conflict between the Ichneumonidae and the caterpillars it preys upon. There too we find a natural evil that benefits the Ichneumonidae while harming the caterpillars it preys upon that so troubled Charles Darwin.[2] This conflict seems perfectly analogous to conflicts that are present virtually whenever and wherever natural evils occur in our world. Assuming that we think that both God and ourselves should leave the Ichneumonidae and the caterpillars it preys upon to work out this conflict on their own, do we want to generalize the solution we reached for that case to all other cases of natural evil? That would mean that both God and ourselves should not interfere with any of these natural evils or their consequences. Yet surely that is not what we think we morally ought to do when facing the impact of natural evils, particularly on other people. Rather, when the basic

© The Author(s) 2019
J. P. Sterba, *Is a Good God Logically Possible?*,
https://doi.org/10.1007/978-3-030-05469-4_8

welfare of other humans is at stake, in particular, we think we ought to prevent such natural evils from occurring or at least prevent or mitigate their consequences, especially when we can easily do so without causing greater harm to other humans.[3]

Happily, this is perfectly consistent with our not taking sides in the conflict between the Ichneumonidae and the caterpillars it preys upon. That is because the conflict between the Ichneumonidae and the caterpillars it preys upon has no significant effect on us, or on any other sentient beings, it seems, one way or the other. So it is perfectly appropriate for us to let the two species work out their conflict on their own. Rather, it would seem that what we are morally required to do is let the Ichneumonidae and the caterpillars alone to work out their conflict as best they can. Maybe in time, caterpillars will evolve a way of effectively defending themselves against these wasps with the result that the Ichneumonidae, if they are to survive, will need to evolve some new means of preying on caterpillars or on other insects. In fact, some of the wasp's would-be prey have developed effective defensive measures.[4] In any case, this conflict between the Ichneumonidae and its prey does not seem to be one where we (or God) should be taking sides.

I

Nevertheless, it is not the case that when human welfare is involved, we should always favor human welfare over the welfare of nonhuman living beings. Elsewhere I have defended a Principle of Disproportionality that places limits on when we could favor human over nonhuman interests.[5] According to this principle:

> Actions that meet nonbasic or luxury needs of humans are prohibited when they aggress against the basic needs of individual animals and plants or even of whole species or ecosystems.

Of course, many people live out their lives in wholesale violation of this principle. Violations are so widespread that we can even imagine that it might take aliens coming to earth to set things right.

Thus, suppose our planet were invaded by an intelligent and very powerful species of aliens who could easily impose their will upon us. Suppose these aliens have studied the life history of our planet and they have come to understand how we have wreaked havoc on our planet, driving many species into extinction, and how we still threaten still many other species with extinction. Suppose further that these aliens are fully aware of the differences between us and the other species on the planet. Suppose they clearly recognize that we more closely resemble them in power and intelligence than any other species on the planet. Even so, suppose the aliens still choose to protect those very species we threaten. Imagine that they force us to use no more resources than we need for a decent life, and this significantly reduces the threat we pose to many endangered species. How then could we object to the actions of these nonhuman species–loving aliens?[6]

Of course, we might argue that there are other more effective ways to protect endangered species, but if the actions of these aliens proved to be the most effective at protecting endangered species, what could our objection be? Moreover, if aliens would be morally justified in constraining our abuse of nonhuman species then surely God would be as well. Even so, this would be just another instance where in virtue of the argument of previous chapters, God should be involved in preventing significant and especially horrendous consequences of human wrongdoing. The only difference is that here the morally wrongful human actions at stake are directed at nonhumans rather than at humans.

II

Nevertheless, the focus of this chapter is on natural, not moral, evil. So the question we need to address is whether God should be preventing, rather than permitting, significant and especially horrendous evil consequences of natural evil upon ourselves and other living beings. Now it is clear that at least when the welfare of other humans is at stake, we think we morally ought to prevent such consequences from occurring, especially when we can easily do so without causing greater harm to other humans.

Yet might things be different for God? Could it be that God by taking the interests of all living beings into account would be exempt from such an obligation? Of course, we too arguably should be taking the interests of all living beings into account as well. However, the practical implications of doing so would seem to be different for us than they are for God. Unlike God, we would be in competition with nonhuman living beings such that our survival and basic well-being requires preferring our own interests to their interests in many cases of conflict.

For God, things, however, would be different. God would not be competing with other living beings. God is presumably above the conflicts his creatures have with each other. So why wouldn't it be morally appropriate for God to take a neutral stand with regard to the conflicts we have with nonhuman living beings and let the natural evils fall where they may, just the way we concluded that it was morally appropriate for us, as well as for God, to remain neutral with regard to the conflict between the Ichneumonidae and the caterpillars it preys upon? Now one might think that if God were not open to a special relationship with us, he might well be neutral with respect to the conflicts between ourselves and other species just as we ourselves if we were not open to a special relationship with our fellow humans might too be neutral with respect to conflicts between our fellow humans and other species. However, given that it is virtually definitive of traditional theism that God is open to just such a special relationship with us, which, when combined with what I have called a Godly opportunity for soul-making, could ultimately include friendship with God himself, then surely God would be morally required to act to prevent significant and especially horrendous evil consequences of natural evil from being inflicted on us when he could easily do so without causing greater harm to other humans.[7]

Moreover, even if it were not definitive of theism that God is open to a special relationship with us, such a relationship, with the protection it would mandate, would still be moral required. This is because meeting our basic needs over those of other species who do not suffer as intensely as we do is the best way to limit serious suffering in the world. A similar moral rationale also supports favoring the basic needs of nonhuman sentient beings over nonsentient living beings, and there is also similar moral rationale for limiting harm to nonsentient living beings when their interests do not conflict with those of any other living beings. All these moral rationales are incorporated into the Natural Evil Prevention Requirements set out below.

So what does this imply about what God should be doing in this regard? Here it would be helpful to appeal to the analogy of a just and powerful political state that was used in earlier chapters. Such a state, it was argued, would not try to prevent all the moral evil that occurs in its domain, even if that were within its power to do so. Instead, it would focus on preventing the significant moral evils that impact people's lives. It would not seek to prevent lesser evils because any general attempt to prevent such evils would tend to interfere with people's significant freedoms.[8] Rather, a just state would leave such evils to be employed by individuals for soul-making as far as possible. Accordingly, it was argued that God, like a just state, should be focused on preventing (not permitting) just the consequences of significant moral evils which impact on others, while leaving wrongdoers the freedom to imagine, intend, and even to take initial steps toward carrying out their wrongdoing.

So here we need to imagine that a just and powerful political state would also be concerned with preventing the significant consequences of natural evils as well as those of moral evils. This extension is a perfectly natural one. In fact, in our own times, we see political states attempting to prevent the consequences of significant natural evils, especially to its own citizens when they are able to do so without causing greater harm to others, either citizens or noncitizens. We saw such efforts by political states and the world community to deal with the Ebola virus and later we saw something similar with respect to the Zika virus. So all we need imagine is that an ideally just and powerful state is technologically proficient enough to deal with most of the significant and even the horrendous consequences of natural evil that we face in our world. Accordingly, with respect to natural evils, such as earthquakes, hurricanes, tornadoes, and floods, we could imagine that an ideally just and powerful state would have extremely accurate warning systems that predicted such disasters years in advance so as to know not to build in certain areas or to build only to specifications that resist the relevant natural disasters. Again, existing political states are already doing this to some extent. We are just imagining ideally just and powerful states doing a superb job preventing significant and especially horrendous consequences of natural evil in order to maintain a special relationship with all those within its domain. So if this is what we would morally expect of ideally just and powerful political states, why would we not expect the same of an all-good, all-powerful God who is seeking to maintain a special relationship with us that could ultimately include friendship?[9]

Now it is clear that our moral concern for preventing harm to others also includes a concern to prevent significant harm to nonhuman sentient beings whenever human welfare is not at stake and we can easily do so without causing greater harm to other nonhuman sentient beings.[10] That is why William Rowe's example of a fawn caught in a forest fire morally troubles us.[11] We think that if we could easily save the fawn from burning to death and human welfare was not at stake, we should do so if we can without causing greater harm to other nonhuman sentient beings. But then, as Rowe claimed, God should do so as well. Of course, many of God's interventions would have to be miraculous, although they do not always have to appear to be such.[12] For example, a sudden rainstorm might suppress a forest fire enabling animals to escape who would otherwise burn to death.

Doubtless, it will be objected that if God were to directly intervene to present significant and especially horrendous consequences of natural evil that would eliminate any need for us to do so ourselves. Thus using a different example than those used in earlier chapters, suppose that you live near a forest preserve where lightening frequently causes forest fires.[13] Suppose during one such fire, you are attempting to help some deer escape who are surrounded by the fire and you use a fire suppressant to open up a path for most, but not all of the deer. Suppose just then God intervenes with a cloud burst suppressing the fire just enough for the rest of the deer to escape. Presumably, you would be happy with God's intervention in such a case.

Yet imagine during another forest fire you are considering whether to intervene again to prevent some deer from being burned alive. You might reason that if you did intervene you might well be completely successful this time. Yet upon further reflection, you might decide that there really is no need for you to do so because if you do nothing, you now assume that God would again intervene as he had done, in part, before to prevent the evil consequences. So you do nothing.

According to some theists, this is just the sort of behavior we would expect if God were to regularly intervene to prevent significant and especially horrendous consequences of natural evils. Hence, they claim, this explains why God does not normally intervene to prevent evil in this way. If God did intervene, on their account, we would lose the motivation we have to intervene and prevent the harmful consequences of the natural evil ourselves, and thereby fail to utilize the opportunities we have for soul-making.

Now I maintain that rather than always intervening or always not intervening God should be engaging in what I would call constrained intervention. To see how this would work, consider again the second case where you decided not to intervene to save s deer from another forest fire on the assumption that God himself would do so, as he had, in part, done before when you were trying your best but were not going to be completely successful at saving all the deer who were surrounded by the fire.

Suppose what happens next is not exactly what you had expected. Yes, God does intervene to save the deer, but that intervention is only partly successful. Originally, let's say, on this second occasion, you yourself were in a position with your new model fire suppressant to save all the deer who were threatened by the flames. Now that you have chosen to do nothing, you see that God eventually brings about a drenching rain but not before some of the deer have been painfully singed by the flames. So you cannot help but note that this second intervention was not as completely successful as it presumably would have been if you had chosen to intervene yourself. After all, you could have saved all the deer without having any of them singed by the fire.

So you begin to detect a pattern. When you choose to intervene to do good yourself, you will either be completely successful or your intervention will fall short. When the latter is going to happen, God does something to make the intervention completely successful.[14] Likewise, when you choose not to intervene when you could do so, God again intervenes but this time not in a fully successful way. In cases of this sort, there is a residue of bad consequences that the victims still do suffer. This residue is not a significant moral violation itself, but it is harmful nonetheless, and it is something for which you are primarily responsible. In our example, you could have provided a warning of impending natural disaster in good time, but you chose not to do so, and that makes you responsible for the consequences. Of course, God too could have saved all the deer without having any of them singed by the flames when you decided not to do so yourself. It is just that in such cases, God has chosen not to fully intervene and completely do what is needed in order to leave you with an opportunity for soul-making. Moreover, I maintain that this is exactly what God would be required to do here: Prevent significant and especially horrendous consequences of natural evil, as needed, to maintain an appropriate moral relationship with his creatures.

It is important to see here that the problem of natural evil and the problem of moral evil are distinct problems and the solution to each of them is importantly different. Thus, with respect to natural evil in our world, it is not possible to avoid all significant natural evil. When a serious flood occurs the would-be victims of the flood and the scavengers who would survive by feeding on their dead bodies are in conflict in our world. One or the other will suffer death. However, with respect to moral evil of the significant and especially the horrendous evil sort, the situation is different. Except for lifeboat cases, individual human beings are not in unavoidable life-and-death conflict with each other. With respect to most of the conflicts we have, morality imposes its demands on each of us such that it is possible for us all to live decent lives together, without anyone doing anything that is significantly or especially horrendously morally evil, thereby imposing significant and possibly horrendous evil consequences on others. This is why it would be possible, and morally required of God, to prevent all the significant and especially horrendous evil consequences of our immoral actions, as needed, at the same time that it would not be possible, and so not morally required of God, to prevent all the significant or even horrendous evil consequences of natural evil in the world. Nevertheless, with respect to natural evil, God would be under a further obligation to prevent significant and especially horrendous consequences of natural evil, as needed, to maintain an appropriate moral relationship with his creatures or to limit serious harm in the world. More specifically, God would be morally required to abide by the following:

Natural Evil Prevention Requirements

I) Prevent, rather than permit, significant and especially horrendous evil consequences of natural evil from being inflicted on rational beings (a good to which they have a right), as needed, when one can easily do so without causing greater or comparable harm to other rational beings.[15]

II) Do not permit, rather than prevent, significant and especially horrendous evil consequences of natural evil to be inflicted on rational beings (which would violate their rights) simply to provide other rational beings with goods they would morally prefer not to have.

III) Do not permit, rather than prevent, significant and especially horrendous evil consequences of natural evils from being inflicted on rational beings (which would violate their rights) in order to provide them with goods to which they do not have a right, when there are countless morally unobjectionable ways of providing those goods to rational beings.

IV) Prevent, rather than permit, significant and especially horrendous evil consequences of natural evil from being inflicted on nonrational sentient beings, as needed, whenever the welfare of rational beings is not at stake and one can easily do so without causing greater or comparable harm to other nonrational sentient life.

V) Do not permit, rather than prevent, significant and especially horrendous evil consequences of natural evil to be inflicted on nonrational sentient beings simply to provide rational beings with goods they would morally prefer not to have.

VI) Do not permit, rather than prevent, significant and especially horrendous evil consequences of natural evils from being inflicted on nonrational sentient beings whenever the welfare of rational beings is not at stake in order to provide nonrational sentient beings with goods not required for their basic welfare, when there are countless morally unobjectionable ways of providing those goods to nonrational sentient beings.

VII) Prevent, rather than permit, significant and especially horrendous evil consequences of natural evil from being inflicted on nonsentient living beings, as needed, whenever the welfare of rational and nonrational sentient beings is not at stake and one can easily do so without causing greater or comparable harm to other nonsentient life.[16]

VIII) Do not permit, rather than prevent, significant and especially horrendous evil consequences of natural evil to be inflicted on nonsentient living beings simply to provide rational beings with goods they would morally prefer not to have.

IX) Do not permit, rather than prevent, significant and especially horrendous evil consequences of natural evils from being inflicted on nonsentient living beings whenever the welfare of rational and nonrational sentient beings is not at stake in order to provide nonsentient living beings with goods not required for their basic welfare, when there are countless morally unobjectionable ways of providing those goods to nonsentient living beings.

Now at least for horrendous consequences of natural evil, Natural Evil Prevention Requirements I–IX apply first to political states, and only when those states either cannot or wrongfully do not meet them, do they apply to the individuals, particularly but not exclusively, to the individuals who are responsible for the actions of those states, and only when such individuals either cannot, or wrongfully do not, meet the requirements do they then apply to God. What this order of application ensures is that as much soul-making obtains as possible consistent with the meeting of these exceptionless minimal natural evil requirements.

It also should be pointed out here that God's interventions to prevent the consequences of significant and especially horrendous natural evil would have a law-like regularity to them. This means that God's intervention to prevent evil consequences in any one case would demand his intervention in all other similar cases. Moreover, the same holds true for political states and their members. Their obligation to prevent evil consequences (including both natural and moral) also has a law-like regularity to them, such that an obligation in one case implies an obligation in other similar cases. Of course, in the case of God, it is the absence of any law-like prevention of the significant and especially the horrendous consequences of natural evil in our world that is logically incompatible with God's existence.

So let us see whether my solution to the problem of natural evil can be undercut by two recent attempts by Michael Murray and Trent Dougherty to provide a theistic solution to that problem.

III

In his book *Nature Red and Tooth and Claw*, Murray explores four possible ways of defending a theistic solution to the problem of natural evil (Murray 2008). The first, tracing its history back to Rene Descartes in the seventeenth century, denies the very existence of animal pain and suffering. However, Murray argues that the best defenders of this approach today no longer deny that animals experience pain and suffering. Instead, they distinguish between different levels of pain and suffering and/or the mental states associated with them, attributing only lower levels to most nonhuman animals. One possibility is that nonhuman animals experience the same pain and suffering that we do but then lack a second-order awareness of that pain and suffer. Yet there are other possibilities as well. Here Murray concludes that it is difficult to show that there are not morally relevant differences between the way we humans experience pain and suffering and the way other nonhuman sentient beings do. Murray goes on to consider whether if there are such morally relevant differences between ourselves and other nonhuman sentient beings, we can still hold that "animals inherently merit moral respect" (Ibid., p. 70). He allows that we can, but only if we "appeal to the fact that the Christian Scriptures portray the natural world as possessing intrinsic worth in virtue of its status as a divine creation" (Ibid., p. 71).

Unfortunately, this way of defending a theistic solution to the problem of natural evil seriously underestimates our ability to come up with defensible reason-based principles for our interacting with nonhuman living beings, such as the biocentric principles for conflict resolution that I have defended elsewhere.[17] These principles do not require that the way we experience pain and suffering match the way that other nonhuman living beings experience pain and suffering in order to morally ground a moral requirement not to inflict pain and suffering on nonhuman sentient beings. For example, all that the Principle of Disproportionality requires in order to prohibit aggression against the basic needs of nonhuman sentient living beings is that the aggression be just for the sake of meeting our own nonbasic or luxury needs. Of course, this is not to deny that the differences between the way that we experience pain and suffering and the way that other nonhuman living beings experience it have some moral relevance. It is just that the moral relevance they have does not undercut the justification that we can give for the six Natural Evil Prevention Requirements defended in this chapter.

Murray's second possible way of defending a theistic solution to the problem of natural evil is to attribute the natural evil, including pre-Adamic animal pain and suffering, to the free evil acts of Satan and his cohorts. However, we already have physical and biological explanations for much of the natural evil from hurricanes to animal pain and suffering. So why should we add another explanatory layer on top of those explanations? Moreover, some of this natural evil, such as that which results from the conflict between the Ichneumonidae and the caterpillars it preys upon is inevitable, and, hence, morally defensible given God's choice to bring such creatures into existence. So are we to imagine that Satan and his cohorts also play a role in bringing about such morally defensible natural evil as well? That makes no sense. More importantly, this way of defending a theistic solution to the problem of natural evil cannot explain why God, when he can easily do so, does not have a moral obligation to prevent significant and especially horrendous consequences of natural evil, even supposing they are caused by Satan and his cohorts, analogous to the way I have argued that God has a moral obligation to prevent significant and especially horrendous immoral consequences that we ourselves cause when he can easily do so.

Murray's third possible way of defending a theistic solution to the problem of natural evil attempts to find an outweighing good that directly benefits nonhuman animals themselves. Here Murray concludes that pain and suffering will be inevitable for nonhuman sentient beings engaged in intentional behavior in our world and to that extent they are morally justified (Murray 2008, p. 121). Yet even granting this is the case, God would still be morally obligated to prevent the significant and especially the horrendous harmful consequences of natural evil as specified by the six Natural Evil Prevention Requirements, which, of course, undermines this third way that Murray wants to defend a theistic solution to the problem of natural evil.[18]

Murray's fourth possible way of defending a theistic solution to the problem of natural evil seeks to show that the nomic regularity of our world and its long development from disorder to order provides outweighing goods that justify God's permission of natural evil, including the pain and suffering of nonhuman sentient beings. Murray tries to support this view by arguing that if God were to prevent any particular instance of pain and suffering of nonhuman sentient beings, he would in consistency have to prevent all similar instances of pain and suffering, and that doing this would seriously disrupt nomic regularity and development from disorder to order of the world and thereby lead to less good overall. No doubt the need for consistency surely holds for cases involving significant and especially horrendous consequences of natural evil that God is obligated to prevent. All such evil consequences should be prevented by God as needed.[19] Nevertheless, there is no reason to think that God's doing this would adversely affect the nomic regularity and development from disorder to order of our world, leading to less good overall, as Murray maintains here.

To see this, we only need to consider the nomic regularity and the development from disorder to order that would obtain in an ideally just and powerful political state and compare that to the nomic regularity and development from disorder to order that would obtain in a significantly unjust, but equally powerful, political state, a state more like the political states in which we actually live. Thus, both political states would exhibit a nomic regularity and a development from disorder to order, but only the nomic regularity and a development from disorder to the order of the ideally just political state would be adequately morally justified.

Similarly, we can imagine the nomic regularity and development from disorder to order that would obtain in a world where God regularly acts, as needed, to prevent significant and especially horrendous consequences of natural evils in accord with the six Natural Evil Prevention Requirements and compare that to the nomic regularity and development from disorder to order that would obtain in a world, like our own. Both worlds would exhibit a nomic regularity and a development from disorder to order, but only the nomic regularity and development from disorder to order of the world in which God would be intervening in accord with six Natural Evil Prevention Requirements would be adequately morally justified. Of course, the nomic regularity and development from disorder in my God-intervening world would conflict with some of the causal regularities with which we are familiar in our world, substituting in their place different regularities, but this would constitute no problem at all for the all-good, all-powerful God of theism whose behavior is constrained only by logic and morality.[20]

In sum, none of Murray's four possible ways of defending a theistic solution to the problem of natural evil undercut the solution I have offered to the problem of natural evil in this chapter. Let us now turn to Trent Dougherty's attempt to defend a theistic solution to the problem of natural evil, or more specifically, the problem of animal pain.

IV

In his book *The Problem of Animal Pain*, Dougherty employs a version of John Hick's theodicy of soul-making in an attempt to provide a God-justifying account of animal suffering (Dougherty 2014).[21] Hick himself did not see his theodicy applying to animals (Hick 1973). Others have agreed. For example, Marilyn Adams holds that humans alone are actual or potential meaning makers in the sense required for soul-making (Adams 1999, p. 28).

Nevertheless, Dougherty thinks he can overcome their objections. Animals, he maintains, will not only be resurrected at the eschaton, but will be deified in much the same way that humans will be. That they will become, in the language of Narnia, "talking animals." Language is the characteristic mark of high intelligence. So [he suggests] that they will become full-fledged persons (rational substances) who can look back on their lives—both pre- and post-personal—and form attitudes about what has happened to them and how they fit into God's plan. If God is just and loving, and if they are rational and of good will, then they will accept, though with no loss of the sense of the gravity of their suffering, that they were an important part of something infinitely valuable, and that in addition to being justly, lavishly rewarded for it, they will embrace their role in creation. In this embrace, [natural] evil is defeated (Dougherty 2014, p. 3).

As we can see, in order to overcome the objections he faces to including animals in an afterlife, Dougherty postulates that animals will experience a drastic augmentation of their powers after they are resurrected. Using those powers, Dougherty claims that animals can then become deified, like humans. Hick, Adams, and others had maintained that animals are not capable of an afterlife as they are. Dougherty agrees. For him, animals become capable of an afterlife only after they have been resurrected and given appropriate powers that transform them into rational agents.

Of course, Dougherty's critics might still object to the idea of God transforming animals into rational agents in an afterlife. To meet this objection, Dougherty provides some biblical support and some support from each of the Eastern Orthodox, Catholic, and Protestant traditions, but the strongest support he provides is philosophical (Ibid., pp. 158–164). He argues that given that God is responsible for the natural evil from which animals suffer, the only way God can compensate for that evil and defeat it is by resurrecting animals and turning them into rational agents who can then engage in soul-making. As Dougherty sees it, his solution to the problem of animal pain simply follows from a correct understanding of what an all-good, all-powerful God would have to do (Ibid., p. 9).

Dougherty goes on to offer two suggestions as to how we might envision his proposed transformation of animal life. One is to view it as analogous to our own transformation from infants to rational agents. He writes:

> What I am suggesting is that we think about non-human animals in essentially the same way we think about infants. The key feature is that we see animals in terms of a developmental spectrum. They are now in an extended infant-like state (or perhaps childlike in the higher phyla) But this is a stage of their development just as it is for the human infant. (Ibid., p. 142)

So just as we can reflect upon painful things that were done to us when we were infants and come to view them as justified from our current perspective as rational agents, so animals whose powers are appropriately transformed in an afterlife could do the same.

Dougherty's other suggestion as to how we might envision his proposed transformation of animal life derives from the C.S. Lewis's *The Chronicles of Narnia* (Lewis 1955). In the first chronicle, a cabby and his work horse, Strawberry, are transported into a land where animals are just having their powers enhanced and where they are gaining the power of speech for the first time. With some effort, Strawberry himself begins to speak:

> you used to tie a horrid black thing behind me and then hit me to make me run, and however far I ran this black thing would always be coming rattle-rattle behind me. (Dougherty 2014, p. 152)

To which the cabby replies:

> We 'ad our living to earn, see … Yours the same as mine. And if there' ad been no work and no whip there'd 'ave been no stable, no mash and no oats. (Ibid., pp. 152–3)

The conversation continues in a similar vein and then breaks off, but the general idea is that if the cabby had really done his best by Strawberry, the horse, realizing this, would surely come around to be reconciled with him in this new world with respect to his previous treatment of the horse.

Dougherty suggests a similar exchange would take place between God and animals in the afterlife once the animals have their powers transformed to make them into rational agents. After the animals have been transformed, if they are of good will, they would come to accept God's permission of natural evil in their lives and in so doing not only would they be compensated for that evil, but through their acceptance of it, the evil itself would be defeated as well (Ibid., p. 153).

According to Dougherty, the "earlier suffering [of animals is] an occasion for their later enhanced selves to make a judgment call about whether they would be glad they were of use to God and fellow creatures or whether they whether to be bitter about it" (Ibid., p. 150). Furthermore, their gladness is supposed to be a manifestation of great virtue and, like the virtue of self-sacrifice, the highest created good (Ibid.) Yet one virtuous act alone does not make someone virtuous. Virtue has to be habitual and requires a pattern of similar behavior. Those who do virtuous deeds usually exhibit a pattern of similar behavior either before or after their virtuous act. So it would take more than one virtuous deed to make enhanced animals virtuous in an afterlife.

Suppose then we were to amend Dougherty's account and assume that animals would have sufficient time in an afterlife, giving them ample opportunities to make themselves virtuous.[22] With that change, would Dougherty's theodicy work for animals?

Clearly, it would make the opportunities that God would be providing to animals in the afterlife similar to the opportunities that God would presumably be providing to us in this life. Hence, the key question is whether the opportunities for soul-making we are provided with in this life are morally justifiable. Or put another way, can God be morally blamed for providing us with just the opportunities we have in this life and nothing more? The opportunities we have in this life are obviously more than the one-off opportunity for soul-making that Dougherty envisions transformed animals having in an afterlife. But are they morally justifiable? Can God be morally blamed for providing us with just the opportunities we have and nothing else?

To see why the opportunities we have are not morally justifiable, consider again our often-used analogy of a just and powerful political state. Such a state would want to restrict our opportunities to do moral evil but it would not want to restrict all such opportunities, even if that were within its power to do so. Instead, it would focus on restricting our opportunities to impose significant and especially horrendous evil the consequences of immoral actions on others. It would not seek to restrict our opportunities to do lesser evil because any general attempt to restrict such opportunities would tend to interfere with our significant opportunities to do morally good actions. Rather, a just state would leave such opportunities to do lesser evil to be used by individuals for soul-making as far as possible.

Now if this is what a just political state would do, then, surely an all-good, all-powerful God would be comparably engaged in restricting our opportunities to impose significant and especially horrendous consequences of immoral actions on others, as needed, while not similarly restricting our opportunities to do lesser evils.

Here it might be objected that such a policy of limited intervention by God would constrain good people from being supervirtuous at the same time that it constrains bad people from being the supervicious. If God is going to restricting our opportunities to impose the consequences of significant and especially horrendous immoral actions on others, then both good people and bad people are going to have their opportunities comparably restricted. That means that good people will not be able to be as virtuous as they could otherwise be if they could respond to the opportunity to inflict the consequences of significant and especially horrendous immoral actions on others by freely refraining from inflicting such consequences on others. It also means that bad people will not be able to be as vicious as they could otherwise be if they could respond to such an opportunity to inflict the consequences of significant and especially horrendous immoral actions on others by freely inflicting such consequences on others.

But is this a problem? Dougherty thinks it is. According to Dougherty, God did not "create Auschwitz in order for there to be saints" (Dougherty 2014, p. 105). However, he does think that God permitted Auschwitz in order for there to be saints of the highest virtue.[23] Yet, therein lies the problem because neither you nor I nor a just state would think that it would be morally justified for us to permit, rather than prevent, people from having the opportunity to inflict significant and especially horrendously evil consequences of moral actions on others (as occurred in Auschwitz) when we could easily do so.

To see why, just ask yourself who would object to God or anyone else depriving people of such opportunities? Of course, bad people might object because such a policy limits them in the exercise of their superviciousness. But there is no reason why God or anyone else should listen to their objection in this regard. What about the good people? Would they object to such a policy? How could they? True, the policy does limit good people in the exercise of their supervirtuousness, but that is just what it takes to protect would-be victims from the significantly evil consequences of the actions of bad people. Surely, good people would find the prevention of the infliction of significantly evil consequences on would-be victims by the supervicious worth the constraint imposed on how supervirtuous they themselves could be. In fact, they should find such tradeoffs not only morally acceptable but also morally required.

Nor would good people ever want to wish away the backup role God would have with regard to their attempts to prevent significant and especially the horrendous consequences of immoral actions. Good people would see this as the only way to guarantee that significant and especially the horrendous consequences of immoral actions will not be inflicted on their would-be victims. They would also welcome their first-responder role in the prevention of evil consequences of immoral actions recognizing that their failure to embrace that role would also render them responsible for at least some of the evil that would be inflicted on innocent victims—something good people surely would not want to be the case.

Dougherty thinks that the risks, pains, and injuries that he has experienced from mountain bike racing were compensated for and defeated by the goods he attained from participating in the sport. He may be right about this. But he also suggests that it was a good thing that the "challenge course" where he once worked as an undergraduate was designed so that there was not much risk of actual physical harm (Dougherty 2014, p. 101). Sporting agencies and governmental actors also seem interested in finding ways to limit serious risks associated with the participation in sports, for example, the long-term risks associated with concussions.

Hence, all the more so should a just and powerful state be interested in restricting our opportunities to inflict significant and especially horrendous evil consequences of immoral actions on others when it can easily do so. From which it follows that an all-good, all-powerful God should also be engaged in restricting our opportunities to inflict significant and especially horrendous evil consequences of immoral actions on others when we do not take effective action in this regard. I also explained how God could interfere in this way without undermining the motivation we would have to use the opportunities available to us to prevent the infliction of significant and especially horrendous evil consequences of immoral actions on others.

In sum, for God to be morally engaged with our world with respect to the moral evil in it, he would have to be preventing significant and especially horrendous evil consequences of our immoral action in accord with the three Moral Evil Prevention Requirements defended in Chaps. 4, 5, 6, and 7.[24] Likewise, for God to be morally engaged with our world with respect to the natural evil in it, he would have to be preventing significant and especially horrendous evil consequences of natural evil in accord with the six Natural Evil Prevention Requirements defended in this chapter. Unfortunately, in our world, this has not happened, and that logically implies that God does not exist.[25]

Notes

1. Let's consider the natural evils on this list and other natural evils like the Ichneumonidae preying on caterpillars "first-order natural evils" and the pain, suffering, death, and other harms they cause "second-order natural evils."

2. See Darwin (1896, Vol. II p. 105). For Darwin, the Ichneumonidae, a type of wasp, was an especially troubling species. This is because this particular wasp seeks out a caterpillar in which to deposit its eggs. It paralyzes but does not kill the caterpillar since a dead and decaying caterpillar would be of no use to its larvae. Then, when its larvae hatch, they are able to feed on the still living caterpillar. The larvae first eat the caterpillar's fat bodies and digestive organs, preserving intact, for last, the essential heart and central nervous system, thereby keeping the caterpillar alive as long as possible as they continue to devour it. Stephen Jay Gould suggests, in what he allows is an inappropriate anthropocentric interpretation, that this pattern of eating "cannot help but recall the ancient English penalty for treason – drawing and quartering, with its explicit object of extracting as much torment as possible by keeping the victim alive and sentient." See Gould (1983, p. 35). For how Darwin's problem of natural evil could be resolved, but only provisional, in a way that is compatible with the existence of God, see Sterba (2019, "Solving Darwin's Problem of Natural Evil").

3. Obviously, when our own interests are being threatened by natural evils we can legitimately try to avert them. This is taken for granted. Hence, the focus here is on the obligations we have particularly to other human beings who are threatened by those evils. Furthermore, our moral concern here should be extended to others who have that same moral status as human beings such as the great apes.

4. See Gould (1983, Chapter 2).

5. See Sterba (2014, Chapter 6).

6. For further exploration of this alien possibility, see (Ibid., pp. 156–158).
7. The other humans are those other humans who either exist or would definitely exist. Humans who just could exist, that is, possible humans, have no moral status here. In addition, for us, the harming that would provide an excuse for not interfering would have to be causal necessitated. For God, the harming would have to be logically, not causally, necessitated since God cannot be subject to causal limitations. Yet it can then be shown that assuming that God is constrained by logical necessity in such contexts leads to a contradiction. For an analogous conclusion regarding moral evil and the argument for it, see Chap. 5.
8. As I indicated in Chap. 2, I am understanding freedoms to be primarily those freedoms a just political state would want to protect since that would fairly secure each person's fundamental interests.
9. Notice too that the only way that a political state could claim that it had failed to prevent significant and especially horrendous evil consequences in the past when it could easily have done so is by allowing that it really wasn't a just political state in the past, and presently is seeking, as best it can, to make up for its past failings. Such as story of repentance and redemption, however, is not one that we can use to explain the actions of the God of theism over time.
10. The other nonhuman sentient beings are those other nonhuman sentient beings who either exist or would definitely exist. Nonhuman sentient beings who just could exist, that is, possible nonhuman sentient beings, have no moral status here.
11. See Rowe (1979, pp. 335–41).
12. The possibility of miracles has never been in question at least in the Judeo-Christian-Islamic tradition. Books of both the Old and New Testaments and the Koran are filled with what are assumed by believers to be miracles. Claims of miracles are made in modern times as well. In recent years, over twelve hundred saints have been canonized in Roman Catholicism, normally requiring two miracles each. Catholic World Report http://www.catholicworldreport.com/Item/2812/the_new_saints_and_blesseds_of_2013.aspx accessed 6/7/18.
   In addition, for Catholics, there is the doctrine of transubstantiation according to which God transforms the substance of bread and wine, the accidents remaining unchanged, into the body and blood of Christ, and, then just when that previous bread and wine would otherwise be broken

down and digested, changes it back into the substance of bread and wine again. This miracle is thought to occur hundreds of thousands of times daily whenever the Roman Catholic Mass is celebrated.

Moreover, the miraculous interventions I am imagining God making are consistent with our natures as they would be realized in a perfectly just and powerful state. By contrast, miraculous interventions that would always keep the lion from eating the zebra or any other living being would change the lion into something else; it would not be consistent with the lion's nature. A change of this sort occurs when we confine lions in zoos, breed them there, and feed them meat from animals they did not hunt and kill themselves.

13. Here I am employing an example involving natural evil.
14. To complicate things here a bit, maybe even in this case, God's intervention should not be completely successful. This is because if we discovered that only when we intervened ourselves, really doing our best, was the intervention completely successful, that could motivate us to always do our best, relying on God for help only when we could do no more ourselves.
15. The "as needed" clause is there to indicate that whether God acts in this regard and the degree to which he does act depend on what we do.
16. The other nonsentient living beings are other nonsentient living beings who either exist or would definitely exist. Nonhuman sentient living beings who just could exist, that is, possible nonhuman sentient beings, have no moral status here. This last condition (requirement) would be violated if God or ourselves attempted to intervene in the conflict between the Ichneumonidae and the caterpillars it preys upon for the purpose of preventing harm to one or the other of them.
17. See Sterba (2014, Chapter 6). Trent Dougherty has also provided a strong argument against neo-Cartesianism in Dougherty (2014, Chapters 4 and 5).
18. Murray considers whether reward in an afterlife may justify God's permission of animal pain and suffering here. I am going to defer consideration of this possible justification because it is at the heart of Dougherty's justification for God's permission of animal pain and suffering which I will take up shortly.
19. A comparable consistency may not be required when God would be acting in a supererogatory way.

20. This is my answer to those who would press the need for nomic regularity against my logical argument against the existence of God, for example, Richard Swinburne; see Swinburne (1998) and Peter van Inwagen (2006). Of course, it is difficult to fully imagine the new regularity that would obtain in our world if God, or an ideally just and powerful state, would intervene in accordance with Moral Evil Prevention Requirements I–III and Natural Evil Prevention Requirements I–IX. Yet one thing we can say for sure is that morally good people would not object to it.

21. I will follow Dougherty in this section and use "animals" to include pretty much all past, present, or future nonhuman sentient beings, all of whose lives involve pain and suffering.

22. It is a bit difficult to imagine how the required soul-making could go on somewhere at the same time for billions upon billions of transformed animals.

23. Dougherty thinks that a foreseen/intended distinction can be used here with respect to God's permission of evil. The idea is that God would not really be intending evil consequences at all but merely foreseeing their occurrence, or, put another way, God would intentionally be doing something, that is, making us free, but then God would only be foreseeing the evil consequences that result therefrom. Yet God is said to be permitting these evil consequences, and permitting is an intentional act. So if God intends not to stop the evil consequences of our actions when he can easily do so then he is not merely foreseeing those consequences.

24. Although these two requirements were defended in both of these chapters, they were only given the name "Moral Evil Prevention Requirements" in Chap. 6.

25. It is worth noting that for Dougherty divine inaction in this world with respect to natural evil, particularly animal pain and suffering, is a serious moral problem. That is why he postulates animal resurrection with a transformation of powers of animals so as to make them into moral agents capable of processing pain and suffering through soul-making in a way that could be morally virtuous. What Dougherty fails to see, however, is that divine inaction with respect to moral evil in our world already logically precludes the existence of God, so the same would be true of divine inaction with respect to the moral evil brought about by these newly constituted rational agents, under Dougherty's hypothesis. That too would logically preclude the existence of God.

Bibliography

Adams, Marilyn. 1999. *Horrendous Evils and the Goodness of God*. Ithaca: Cornell University Press.

Catholic World Report. http://www.catholicworldreport.com/Item/2812/the_new_saints_and_blesseds_of_2013.aspx

Darwin, Frances. 1896. *The Life and Letters of Charles Darwin*. New York: D. Appleton and Company.

Dougherty, Trent. 2014. *The Problem of Animal Pain*. New York: Palgrave Macmillan.

Gould, Stephen Jay. 1983. *Hens Teeth and Horse's Toes*. New York: Norton and Co.

Hick, John. 1973. *Philosophy of Religion*. 2nd ed. Englewood Cliffs: Prentice-Hall.

Lewis, C.S. 1955. *The Chronicles of Narnia: The Magician Nephew*. New York: Harper-Collins.

Murray, M. 2008. *Nature Red in Tooth and Claw*. Oxford: Oxford University Press.

Rowe, William. 1979. The Problem of Evil and Some Varieties of Atheism. *American Philosophical Quarterly* 16: 335–341.

Sterba, James P. 2014. *From Rationality to Equality*. Oxford: Oxford University Press.

———. 2019. Solving Darwin's Problem of Natural Evil. *Sophia*. https://doi./org/10.1007/s11841-019-0704-y. pp.1–12.

Swinburne, R. 1998. *Providence and the Problem of Evil*. Oxford: Clarendon Press.

van Inwagen, P. 2006. *The Problem of Evil*. Oxford: Oxford University Press.

9

Conclusion

In this book, I have drawn on untapped resources in ethics that have proved useful in resolving the problem of evil that has long troubled theists and atheists alike. Those resources cluster around the Pauline Principle that is at the heart of the Doctrine of Double Effect. The foreseen/intended distinction, which is also at the heart of the Doctrine of Double Effect and features prominently in some trolley cases, does not, however, have a role in resolving the problem of evil because God is thought to be constantly sustaining everything that happens and so he never just foresees anything he creates and sustains in existence. Accordingly, the foreseen, but not intended, justification that is involved in a number of trolley cases never applies to God. Nevertheless, some trolley cases, such as Bernard Williams's case of shooting one of twenty Indians in the Amazon to save the remaining nineteen, does not use the foreseen/intended distinction. It is such cases that attempt to justify intentionally doing evil that good may come of it, and this is just the kind of justification that is required for a theistic solution to the problem of evil. Accordingly, most of this book was an attempt to determine whether such a justification exists for the God of traditional theism.

© The Author(s) 2019
J. P. Sterba, *Is a Good God Logically Possible?*,
https://doi.org/10.1007/978-3-030-05469-4_9

In this chapter, I will review the argument of my book in four different ways. First, I will present the conclusions of my argument chapter by chapter paralleling the approach that I used in the Introduction. Second, I will give the basic moral requirements that my argument uses. Third, I will provide a relatively concise statement of the three main sub-arguments of the book: the first from the moral evil in the world, the second from the natural evil in the world, and the third from the lack of God's law-like prevention of evil, as needed, in the world. All three sub-arguments conclude to the logical impossibility of God. The third sub-argument, however, is actually included in the first two because God's prevention of significant and especially horrendous consequences of both moral and natural evil must have a law-like character to it, such that it would apply, as needed, in all relevantly similar circumstances. Still, the third sub-argument usefully focuses on how that law-like prevention would obtain if God were to exist. Finally, I will present my main argument from moral evil in a way that would have enabled John Mackie to succeed in his debate with Alvin Plantinga.

I

Let's begin with the chapter conclusions:

Chapter 2: There Is No Free-Will Defense
In Chap. 2, I argued that there is no Free-Will Defense for the degree and amount of moral evil in our world, but allow that God's creating our world with all the evil in it might still be justified on other grounds.

Chapter 3: An Attempt at Theodicy
In Chap. 3, I explored some of the possible candidates, other than freedom, for justifying God's permission of significant and especially horrendous consequences of immoral actions and found them all wanting.

Chapter 4: The Pauline Principle and the Just Political State
In Chap. 4, I determined that the Pauline Principle and the analogy of an ideally just political state are logically inconsistent with what, if God existed, would have to be God's widespread permission of significant and especially horrendous evil consequences of immoral actions.

Chapter 5: Skeptical Theism to the Rescue?
In Chap. 5, I determined that skeptical theism by failing to adequately take into account the exceptionless minimal requirements of the Pauline Principle also fails to defend traditional theism against a logical argument from evil that utilizes those fundamental requirements of our morality.

Chapter 6: What If God Is Not a Moral Agent?
In Chap. 6, I determined that we cannot consistently drop the assumption that God is a moral agent.[1] Nor is Brian Davies right, I argued, in claiming that this is Aquinas's view. I further determined that Aquinas's own view cannot avoid the logical argument against the existence of God that I developed in previous chapters.

Chapter 7: What About a Redemptive God?
In Chap. 7, I showed that a justification for God's involvement with the evil in the world cannot be found in the long biblical history of God's seeking to bring redemption to a wayward humanity.

Chapter 8: Taking Natural Evil into Account
In Chap. 8, I provided a logical argument from natural evil that parallels the logical argument from moral evil that I developed in preceding chapters.

Chapters 5, 6, and 7 each begins by addressing different objections to the combined arguments of Chaps. 2, 3, and 4 with respect to the degree and amount of moral evil in our world. These chapters not only meet these different objections, but go on to further develop and expand upon the argument of those earlier chapters.

II

Turning to my second way of reviewing my argument, here are the basic moral requirements that my argument uses, all of which are exceptionless minimal components of the Pauline Principle never do evil that good may come of it which are acceptable to consequentialists and nonconsequentialists and are, or should be, acceptable as theists and atheists alike.

Moral Evil Prevention Requirements

I) Prevent, rather than permit, significant and especially horrendous evil consequences of immoral actions without violating anyone's rights (a good to which we have a right), as needed, when that can easily be done.

II) Do not permit significant and especially horrendous evil consequences of immoral actions simply to provide other rational beings with goods they would morally prefer not to have.

III) Do not permit, rather than prevent, significant and especially horrendous evil consequences of immoral actions on would-be victims (which would violate their rights) in order to provide them with goods to which they do not have a right, when there are countless morally unobjectionable ways of providing those goods (Chaps. 2, 3, 4, 5, 6, and 7).

Natural Evil Prevention Requirements

I) Prevent, rather than permit, significant and especially horrendous evil consequences of natural evil from being inflicted on rational beings (a good to which they have a right), as needed, when one can easily do so without causing greater or comparable harm to other rational beings.[2]

II) Do not permit significant and especially horrendous evil consequences of natural evil to be inflicted on rational beings (which would violate their rights) simply to provide other rational beings with goods they would morally prefer not to have.

III) Do not permit, rather than prevent, significant and especially horrendous evil consequences of natural evils from being inflicted on rational beings (which would violate their rights) in order to provide them with goods to which they do not have a right, when there are countless morally unobjectionable ways of providing those goods to rational beings.

IV) Prevent, rather than permit, significant and especially horrendous evil consequences of natural evil from being inflicted on nonrational sentient beings, as needed, whenever the welfare of rational beings is not at stake and one can easily do so without causing greater or comparable harm to other nonrational sentient life.

V) Do not permit significant and especially horrendous evil consequences of natural evil to be inflicted on nonrational sentient beings simply to provide rational beings with goods they would morally prefer not to have.

VI) Do not permit, rather than prevent, significant and especially horrendous evil consequences of natural evils from being inflicted on nonrational sentient beings whenever the welfare of rational beings is not at stake in order to provide nonrational sentient beings with goods not required for their basic welfare, when there are countless morally unobjectionable ways of providing those goods to nonrational sentient beings.

VII) Prevent, rather than permit, significant and especially horrendous evil consequences of natural evil from being inflicted on nonsentient living beings, as needed, whenever the welfare of rational and nonrational sentient beings is not at stake and one can easily do so without causing greater or comparable harm to other nonsentient life.[3]

VIII) Do not permit significant and especially horrendous evil consequences of natural evil to be inflicted on nonsentient living beings simply to provide rational beings with goods they would morally prefer not to have.

IX) Do not permit, rather than prevent, significant and especially horrendous evil consequences of natural evils from being inflicted on nonsentient living beings whenever the welfare of rational and nonrational sentient beings is not at stake in order to provide nonsentient living beings with goods not required for their basic welfare, when there are countless morally unobjectionable ways of providing those goods to nonsentient living beings. (Chap. 8)

Turning to my third way of reviewing my argument, here is a relatively concise statement of the three main sub-arguments of the book.

A) Argument from the Moral Evil in the World

1. Goods that could be provided to us are of just two types. They are either goods to which we have a right or goods to which we do not have a right. (Chaps. 5 and 6)

2. Goods of either of these two types can be first-order goods that do not logically presuppose the existence of some serious wrongdoing or second-order goods that do logically presuppose the existence of some serious wrongdoing. (Chap. 6)

So let us consider each of these four exclusive types of goods in turn.

(a) With Respect to First-Order Goods to Which We Have a Right

3. With respect to first-order goods to which we have a right, such as freedom from brutal assault, God would never be causally stuck, as we sometimes are, in situations where we can only provide some with such a good by not providing others with such a good. God would always have the power to provide both goods in such cases and thereby prevent the evils that would otherwise occur. (Chaps. 4 and 5)

4. Nor could it be logically impossible for God to provide both goods in such cases because that supposition leads to a contradiction. (Chap. 5)

5. Since then God would be facing no causal or logical constraints with respect to providing us with first-order goods to which we have a right, God should always, in virtue of Moral Evil Prevention Requirement I, have provided us with such goods and thereby prevented the evils that would otherwise occur. (Chaps. 4, 5, and 6)

6. But this clearly has not happened because there are significant and especially horrendous evil consequences of immoral actions that, if God exists, would have to have resulted from God's widespread violation of Moral Evil Prevention Requirement I, which is logically incompatible with God's existence, unless there is some other justification for God's permitting those evil consequences. (Chaps. 4, 5, and 6)

(b) With Respect to Second-Order Goods to Which We Have a Right

7. Likewise, with respect to second-order goods to which we have a right, such as receiving needed medical aid after being brutally assaulted, the beneficiaries of such goods would morally prefer

that God had prevented the wrongdoing upon which the provision of those goods logically depends, and so God would have been morally required to do so in virtue of Moral Evil Prevention Requirement II, with the result that, if God existed, there would be no second-order goods to which we have a right. (Chaps. 5 and 6)

8. But this clearly has not happened because there are second-order goods to which we have a right, like receiving needed medical aid after being brutally assaulted, which is also logically incompatible with God's existence in virtue of Moral Evil Prevention Requirement II, unless there is some other justification for God's permitting those evil consequences. (Chaps. 5 and 6)

9. So if God exists, there would have to be some justification for his not preventing significant and especially horrendous evil consequences of immoral actions in such cases other than in terms of first-order goods to which we have a right or second-order goods to which we have a right. (Chaps. 5 and 6)

10. Now the only other possible justification for God's permitting significant and especially horrendous evil consequences of immoral actions would have to be to provide us with first- and second-order goods to which we do not have a right. (Chaps. 4, 5, and 6)

    (c) With Respect to First-Order Goods to Which We Do Not Have a Right

11. With respect to first-order goods to which we do not have a right, God would never be causally constrained by the lack of resources, as we sometimes are, and thereby be unable to provide us with goods to which we do not have a right without permitting significant and especially horrendous evil consequences of immoral actions. (Chap. 5)

12. Nor could it be logically impossible for God to provide such goods without violating our rights by permitting the consequences of significant and especially horrendous immoral actions to be inflicted on us because that supposition leads to a contradiction. (Chap. 5)

13. Since then God would be facing no causal or logical constraints with respect to providing with us with first-order goods to which we do not have a right, God, if he exists, should always have provided us with such goods without violating Moral Requirement III. (Chaps. 4, 5, and 6)

14. That clearly has not happened because there are significant and especially horrendous consequences of immoral action that would have to have resulted from God's widespread violation of Moral Evil Prevention Requirement III, AND THAT IS LOGICALLY INCOMPATIBLE WITH GOD'S EXISTENCE. (Chaps. 4, 5, and 6)

   (d) With Respect to Second-Order Goods to Which We Do Not Have a Right

15. Likewise, with respect to second-order goods to which we do not have a right, like having the opportunity to provide medical aid to someone who has been brutally assaulted, beneficiaries of such goods would morally prefer that God had prevented the wrongdoing upon which the provision of these goods logically depends, and so in accord with Moral Evil Prevention Requirement II, God would have been morally required to do so, with the result that there would be no such second-order goods to which we do not have a right. (Chaps. 5 and 6)

16. But that clearly has not happened because there are such second-order goods to which we do not have a right in virtue of Moral Evil Prevention Requirement II, AND THAT IS LOGICALLY INCOMPATIBLE WITH GOD'S EXISTENCE. (Chaps. 5 and 6)

B) Argument from the Natural Evil in the World

   1. Natural Evil Prevention Requirements I–IX would have to be met by God, if he exists, analogously to the way Moral Evil Prevention Requirements I–III have to be met. (Chap. 8)

   2. Accordingly, the significant and especially horrendous consequences of natural evil that exists in the world would BE LOGICALLY INCOMPATIBLE WITH GOD'S EXISTENCE. (Chap. 8)

C) Argument from the Lack of God's Law-like Prevention of Evil

1. Now it is possible to integrate our having adequate opportunities for soul-making to prevent evil ourselves with God's always preventing significant and especially horrendous evil consequences of moral and natural evil as needed. (Chaps. 4, 5, 6, and 8)

2. But this has not happened, AND THAT IS LOGICALLY INCOMPATIBLE WITH GOD'S EXISTENCE. (Chaps. 2, 3, 4, 5, 6, 7, and 8)

3. Furthermore, although an ideally just and powerful state would do its best to abide by Moral Evil Prevention Requirement I–III and Natural Evil Prevention Requirements I–IX, only God, if he exists, could and should insure, as needed, with law-like regularity, that there would be no significant and especially no horrendous consequences of moral and natural evil inflicted on their victims in violation of these requirements, and hence no second-order goods that would otherwise result from such evil consequences. (Chaps. 2, 3, 4, 5, 6, 7, and 8)

4. But this has not happened, AND THAT IS LOGICALLY INCOMPATIBLE WITH GOD'S EXISTENCE. (Chaps. 2, 3, 4, 5, 6, 7, and 8)

Finally, I will show how the core of my Argument from the Moral Evil in the World can be incorporated into the argument that John Mackie should have used to succeed in his debate with Alvin Plantinga. Mackie's argument which focuses on the moral evil in the world should have proceeded as follows:

1. There is an all-good, all-powerful God. (This is assumed for the sake of argument by both Mackie and Plantinga.)

2. If there is an all-good, all-powerful God then necessarily he would be adhering to Evil Prevention Requirements I–III. (This is because these requirements are exceptionless, minimal components of the Pauline Principle that are acceptable to consequentialists and nonconsequentialists, and are, or should be, acceptable to theists and atheists as well.) See Chaps. 4, 5, and 6.

3. If God were adhering to Evil Prevention Requirements I–III, then necessarily significant and especially horrendous evil consequences of

immoral actions would not be obtaining through what would have to be his permission. (This is established by my Argument from the Moral Evil in the World.)

4. Significant and especially horrendous evil consequences of immoral actions do obtain all around us. (This is assumed by both Mackie and Plantinga.)
5. Therefore, it is not the case that there is an all-good, all-powerful God.

Having thus set out the argument of my book in these different ways, it should be easier to detect any flaw in it.

III

Now this book has focused on bringing ethics to bear on the problem of evil. The main result has been a logical argument against the existence of God based on exceptionless minimal components of the Pauline Principle and on the analogy of an ideally just and powerful political state. As it so happens, J.L. Schellenberg has also put forward a logical argument against the existence of God that brings ethics to bear on the problem of why an all-loving God has not made himself known to finite persons who are nonresistantly in a state of nonbelief with respect to his existence. Schellenberg calls this the problem of divine hiddenness.

Schellenberg claims that this problem emerged only about twenty years ago mainly as the result of his own work, with few philosophical precursors (Schellenberg 2015, pp. vii and Chapter 3). Clearly Schellenberg's argument addressing the divine hiddenness problem has generated a considerable response among philosophers. As he notes:

Articles on the hiddenness argument have now appeared many times over nor only in philosophy journals and books but also in the various Companions and Handbooks on the philosophy of religion put out by presses such as Oxford Cambridge, Routledge and Wiley-Blackwell, and in the Macmillan, Routledge and Stanford encyclopedias of philosophy. The argument ... is moreover frequently seen in discussion of the existence of God on line. It looks to be here to stay. (Ibid., viii)

Nevertheless, the only way a problem of divine hiddenness can get going in the first place is if we assume that the problem of evil has not yet been resolved against theism.[4] This would mean that if my logical argument against the existence of God based on the problem of evil works, it would no longer make sense to go on to raise a problem of divine hiddenness.[5]

Still, another purportedly logical argument against the existence of God assumes that God is a perfect being, and that as such, if he creates at all, he would have to create the best possible world.[6] Yet the world we have is not the best possible world, so the argument goes, because it would be possible to make this world better than it is, for example, by just adding a few more good creatures to it. Hence, the existence of an all-perfect God is not logically compatible with the world as it is.

Yet before God creates, he is not under any obligation to anyone, nor would it benefit anyone, not even himself, to create one particular world rather than any other. Moreover, provided that the creatures in the world that God creates are better off existing than not existing, no one would be harmed by God's creating that particular world rather than any other. After creation, however, God would have an obligation to protect and benefit those he created, but that obligation is grounded in the needs of the creatures he has brought into existence. Hence, given that creatures that exist in this world are almost all, as far as we can tell, better off existing than not existing, there is no argument against the existence of God that can be based on creation. That is why my argument is based on what God would have to be doing after creation because only then would God through his actions be benefiting or harming the creatures he presumptively has made.[7]

So what is a theist to do when faced with the argument of this book that the existence of an all-good, all-powerful God is logically incompatible primarily with exceptionless minimal components of the Pauline Principle, that is, with the three Moral Evil Prevention Requirements and the six Natural Evil Prevention Requirements, together with the analogy of an ideally just and powerful political state. The answer is clear. This argument is obviously new, drawing as it does on previously untapped resources in ethics. So the argument could well have a fatal flaw in it somewhere. What the theists should do then is find that flaw if it exists. Such has always been the way of philosophers, whether they happened to be theists or atheists, at least since the time of Socrates. There surely is no better response that theists could make when faced with my argument.[8]

Yet might it not help to avoid the conclusion of my logical argument against the existence of an all-good, all-powerful God to hypothesize a limited god? This has been an option favored by, among others, by Alfred North Whitehead and Charles Hartshorne (Whitehead 1926; Hartshorne 1967). Unfortunately, such a god would have to be either extremely immoral or extremely weak. Such a god would either have to be extremely immoral, more immoral than all of our historical villains taken together, because he would have permitted all the horrendous evil consequences of those villains when he could easily have prevented them without permitting a greater evil or failing to provide us some greater good. Alternatively, such a god, while morally good, would have to be extremely weak either because he is incapable of preventing the evil consequences that we are only causally incapable of preventing or because he is incapable of providing us with goods to which we are not entitled without permitting us to suffer significant and especially horrendous evil consequences of immoral actions, something that we ourselves are only sometimes causally incapable of doing. Surely then no useful purpose would be served by hypothesizing such a limited god who would either *be so much more evil* than all our greatest villains or, while moral, would *be so much less powerful* than ourselves. Rather, what theists need do is find some fatal flaw in my logical argument from evil against the existence of an all-good, all-powerful God. In this endeavor, in light of my own past struggles with the problem of evil, I can only wish them well.[9]

Notes

1. I further argued that even if we drop the assumption, we still face the conclusion that what would be God's behavior in the world parallels that of our worst villains.
2. The "as needed" clause is there to indicate that whether God acts in this regard and the degree to which he does act depend on what we do.
3. The other nonsentient living beings are other nonsentient living beings who either exist or would definitely exist. Nonhuman sentient living beings who just could exist, that is, possible nonhuman sentient beings, have no moral status here. This last condition (requirement) would be

violated if God or ourselves attempted to intervene in the conflict between the Ichneumonidae and the caterpillars it preys upon for the purpose of preventing harm to one or the other of them.

4. This is because the obligation to prevent (serious) evil has priority over the obligation to do good (which is not itself the prevention of an evil). Accordingly, it would only be possible for a God who has not failed in his obligation not to do (or permit) especially horrendous evil consequences of immoral actions to be inflicted on us to reveal himself by extending an offer of loving friendship to us (something to which we do not have a right). So we can only consider whether it would be appropriate for God to extend such an offer to us if we had assumed that God had not failed in his obligation not to do (or permit) especially horrendous evil consequences of immoral actions to be inflicted on us.

5. Of course, if we were to assume that the problem of evil has not been resolved against theism (that is, if we had not yet determined that God had failed in his obligation not to do (or permit) especially horrendous evil consequences of immoral action to be inflicted on us), then it would make sense to try to raise a logical argument against the existence of God based on divine hiddenness. Of course, part of the justification for doing this would be that the main argument of my book does not work.

6. This argument attempts to turn Leibniz's theodicy into an atheodicy.

7. In Chapter 12 of his *The Nonexistence of God*, Nicholas Evert makes some useful remarks toward offering a logical argument against theism based on the problem of evil. However, he doesn't sketch out the theistic view sufficiently to show how such an argument would have to go. He also may have been writing too early to take into account some more recent defenses of theism with respect to the problem of evil such as that of skeptical theism (Evert 2004).

8. It is worth noting that there are other purported logical arguments against the existence of God. These arguments attempt to derive a logical contradiction from some conception of a would-be divine attribute like omnipotence or omniscience. The problem with such arguments, as even some defenders of atheism have recognized, is that defenders of theism usually can find some modified conception of the divine attribute in question that avoids the contradiction at issue. See Stenger (2007, pp. 30–34). By contrast, with respect to the problem of evil, the fundamental requirements of morality, the violation of which would result in significant and especially horrendous evil, cannot be similarly just defined away. So a logical argument against the existence of God based on the problem of evil

has a clear advantage over other logical arguments based on conceptions of divine attributes other than moral goodness.

9. At age fourteen, I joined the Christian Brothers, a Catholic religious order, and, of course, was a committed theist. When I was twenty-six, I left the Christian Brothers before taking final vows in order to pursue a full-time philosophy PhD program at the University of Pittsburgh. Sometime during my graduate years at Pitt, after doing an independent study on the problem of evil, I became openly agnostic. However, it was only in 2013 after receiving a grant from the John Templeton Foundation that I was able to fully bring my years of working in ethics and political philosophy to bear on the problem of evil. This book, with its logical argument against the existence of God, is the main result.

Bibliography

Evert, Nicholas. 2004. *The Nonexistence of God*. New York: Routledge.

Hartshorne, Charles. 1967. *A Natural Theology for our Time*. La Salle: Open Court.

Schellenberg, J.L. 2015. *The Hiddenness Argument*. Oxford: Oxford University Press.

Stenger, Victor. 2007. *God: The Failed Hypothesis*. Amherst: Prometheus.

Whitehead, Alfred. 1926. *Religion in the Making*. New York: Macmillan.

Further Readings

Adams, Robert Merrihew. 1999. *Finite and Infinite Goods: A Framework for Ethics*. New York: Oxford University Press.

Adams, Marilyn. 2011. Julian of Norwich: Problems of Evil and the Seriousness of Sin. *Philosophia* 39: 433–447.

———. 2013. Ignorance, Instrumentality, Compensation and the Problem of Evil. *Sophia* 52: 7–26.

Adams, Marilyn, and Robert Adams, eds. 1990. *The Problem of Evil*. New York: Oxford University Press.

Alexander, David. 2012. *Goodness, God and Evil*. New York: Continuum International Publishing Group.

Almeida, M., and G. Oppy. 2003. Sceptical Theism and Evidential Argument from Evil. *Australasian Journal of Philosophy* 81: 496–516.

Alston, William. 1991. *Perceiving God*. Ithaca: Cornell University Press.

Andrew of Neufchateau. 1997. *Questions on an Ethics of Divine Commands*. Trans. Janine Idziak. Notre Dame: University of Notre Dame Press.

Audi, Robert, and William Wainwright, eds. 1986. *Rationality, Religious Belief, and Commitment*. Ithaca: Cornell University Press.

Barry William, S.J. 2008. *A Friendship Like No Other: Experiencing God's Amazing Embrace*. Chicago: Loyola Press.

Bergmann, Michael. 1999. Might-Counterfactuals, Transworld Untrustworthiness and Plantinga's Free Will Defense. *Faith and Philosophy* 16 (3): 336–351.

© The Author(s) 2019
J. P. Sterba, *Is a Good God Logically Possible?*,
https://doi.org/10.1007/978-3-030-05469-4

———. 2012. Commonsense Skeptical Theism. In *Reason, Metaphysics and Mind: New Essays on the Philosophy of Alvin Plantinga*, ed. K. Clark and M. Rea. New York: Oxford University Press.

Bergmann, Michael, Michael Murray, and Michael Rea, eds. 2011. *Divine Evil? The Moral Character of the God of Abraham*. Oxford: Oxford University Press.

Betenson, Toby. 2015. Ivan Karamazov Is a Hopeless Romantic. *International Journal for Philosophy of Religion* 77: 65–73.

Bishop, John, and Ken Perszyk. 2011. The Normatively Relativized Logical Argument from Evil. *International Journal of Philosophy of Religion* 70 (2): 109–126.

Boyd, Gregory. 2001. *Satan and the Problem of Evil*. Downer Groves: InterVarsity Press.

Brown, Christopher M. 2015. Making the Best Even Better: Modifying Rawl and Timpe's Solution to the Problem of Heavenly Afterlife. *Faith and Philosophy* 1: 2015.

Buchanan, Alan, and Dan Brock. 1989. *Deciding for Others: The Ethics of Surrogate Decision-Making*. Cambridge: Cambridge University Press.

Burrell, David. 2008. *Deconstructing Theodicy: Why Job Has Nothing to Say to the Puzzle of Suffering*. Grand Rapids: Brazos Press.

Callahan, Laura. 2016. On the Problem of Paradise. *Faith and Philosophy* 2: 2016.

Carrier, Richard. 2014. *On the Historicity of Jesus*. Sheffield: Sheffield Phoenix Press.

Cathcart, Thomas. 2013. *The Trolley Problem*. New York: Workman.

Citron, Gabriel. 2015. Dreams, Nightmares, and a Defense Against Arguments from Evil. *Faith and Philosophy* 3: 247–270.

Coughlan, Michael. 1979. Moral Evil Without Consequences. *Analysis* 39: 58–60.

Crenshaw, James. 2005. *Defending God*. Oxford: Oxford University Press.

Darwin, Frances. 1896. *The Life and Letters of Charles Darwin*. New York: D. Appleton and Company.

Darwin, Charles. 2002. *Autobiographies*. New York: Penguin Books.

Davis, Stephen. 2001. *Encountering Evil*. Louisville: Westminster John Knox Press.

Dawkins, Richard. 1996. *The Blind Watchmaker*. New York: W.W. Norton.

———. 2008. *The God Delusion*. New York: Bantam Books.

De La Puente, Luis S.J. 1951. *God's Friendship*. Trans. John Thrill. Milwaukee: The Bruce.

DeGrazia, David. 2012. *Creation Ethics: Reproduction, Genetics, and Quality of Life*. New York: Oxford University Press.

Dennett, Daniel. 2007. *Breaking the Spell*. New York: Penguin.

DeRose, Keith. 1991. Plantinga, Presumption, Possibility, and the Problem of Evil. *Canadian Journal of Philosophy* 21: 497–512.

Draper, P. 2005. God, Science, and Naturalism. In *The Oxford Handbook of Philosophy of Religion*, ed. William J. Wainwright, Oxford Reference Library of Philosophy, Paul K. Moser. Oxford: Oxford University Press.

———. 2009. The Problem of Evil. In *The Oxford Handbook of Philosophical Theology*, ed. Thomas P. Flint and Michael Rea. Oxford: Oxford University Press.

Draper, Paul, and Trent Dougherty. 2013. Explanation and the Problem of Evil. In *The Blackwell Companion to the Problem of Evil*, ed. Justin McBrayer and Daniel Howard-Snyder, 71–87. Malden: Wiley.

Ehrman, B. 2008. *God's Problem*. New York: Harper-Collins.

———. 2016. *Jesus Before the Gospels*. New York: HarperCollins.

Faden, Ruth, and Tom L. Beauchamp. 1986. *A History and Theory of Informed Consent*. New York: Oxford University Press.

Fales, Evan. 2010. *Divine Intervention*. New York: Routledge.

Feinberg, John. 1994. *The Many Faces of Evil*. Grand Rapids: Zondervan Publishing House.

Frances, Bryan. 2013. *Gratuitous Suffering and the Problem of Evil*. New York: Routledge.

Furlong, Peter. 2014. Is God the Cause of Sin? *Faith and Philosophy* 4: 422–434.

Garrard, Eve, and Geoffrey Scarre. 2003. *Moral Philosophy and the Holocaust*. Burlington: Ashgate Publishing.

Geisler, Norman. 2011. *If God, Why Evil?* Bloomington: Bethany House Publishers.

Geivett, R. Douglas. 1993. *Evil and the Evidence for God*. Philadelphia: Temple University Press.

Gelinas, L. 2009a. The Problem of Natural Evil I. *Philosophy Compass* 4: 533–559.

———. 2009b. The Problem of Natural Evil II. *Philosophy Compass* 4: 560–574.

Gellman, Jerome. 2015. On a New Logical Problem of Evil. *Faith and Philosophy* 4: 439–452.

———. 2017. A Surviving Version of the Common Sense Problem of Evil: A Reply to Tweedt. *Faith and Philosophy* 1: 82–92.

Gould, Stephen Jay. 1983. *Hens Teeth and Horse's Toes*. New York: Norton.

Griffin, David Ray. 1991. *Evil Revisited*. Albany: State University of New York Press.

Hanink, James, ed. 2013. *Aquinas and Maritain on Evil*. Washington, DC: Catholic University of America.

Hare, John. 2007. *God and Morality*. Malden: Blackwell Publishing.

Harris, Sam. 2004. *End of Faith*. New York: W.W. Norton.

Hasker, W. 2004. *Providence, Evil, and the Openness of God*. London: Routledge.
———. 2008. *God's Triumph Over Evil*. Downers Grove: Intervarsity Press.
———. 2010. Defining 'Gratuitous Evil': A Response to Alan R. Rhoda. *Religious Studies* 46: 303–309.
Hick, John. 1966. *Evil and the God of Love*. 2nd ed. New York: Harper & Row.
Himma, Kenneth. 2010. Plantinga's Version of the Free-Will Argument: The Good and Evil That Free Beings Do. *Religious Studies* 46: 21–39.
———. 2016. The Ethics of Subjection a Child to the Risk of Eternal Torment: A Reply to Shawn Bawaulske. *Faith and Philosophy* 1: 94–108.
Hitchens, Christopher. 2007. *God Is Not Great*. New York: Twelve Books.
Howard-Snyder, Daniel, ed. 1996. *The Evidential Argument from Evil*. Bloomington: Indiana University Press.
———. 2009. Epistemic Humility, Arguments from Evil, and Moral Skepticism. In *Oxford Studies in Philosophy of Religion*, ed. J. Kvanvig, vol. 2. Oxford: Oxford University Press.
———. 2013a. The Argument from Inscrutable Evil. In His *The Evidential Argument From Evil*, 286–310. Bloomington: Indiana University Press.
———. 2013b. The Logical Problem of Evil. In *The Blackwell Companion to the Problem of Evil*, ed. Justin McBrayer and Daniel Howard-Snyder. Malden: John Wiley and Sons.
Howard-Snyder, Daniel, and Frances Howard-Snyder. 1994. How an Unsurpassable Being Can Create a Surpassable World. *Faith and Philosophy* 11: 260–268.
Howard-Snyder, Daniel, and Paul Moser, eds. 2002. *Divine Hiddenness*. Cambridge: Cambridge University Press.
Howard-Snyder, Daniel, and John O'Leary-Hawthorne. 1998. Transworld Sanctity and Plantinga's Free Will Defense. *International Journal for Philosophy of Religion* 44: 1–21.
Hume, David. 1948. *Dialogues Concerning Natural Religion*. New York: Hafner Publishing Co.
Joad, C.E.M. 1941. *God and Evil*. New York: Harper and Brothers Publishing.
Jordan, Jeff. 2006. Does Skeptical Theism Lead to Moral Skepticism? *Philosophy and Phenomenological Research* 72: 403–417.
Josephus, Flavius. 1984. *The Jewish War*. New York: Penguin.
Journet, Charles. 1963. *The Meaning of Evil*. Trans. Michael Barry. New York: P.J. Kenedy and Sons.
Julian of Norwich. 1978. *Showings*. Trans. O.S.A. Edmund Colledge, and S.J. James Walsh. Mahwah: Paulist Press.
Kellenberger, James. 2017. *God's Goodness and God's Evil*. Lanham: Lexington Books.

Keller, James. 2007. *Problems of Evil and the Power of God*. Burlington: Ashgate Publishing.

Kelly, Joseph. 2002. *The Problem of Evil in the Western Tradition*. Collegeville: The Liturgical Press.

Knasas, John. 2013. *Aquinas and the Cry of Rachel*. Washington, DC: Catholic University Press.

Kretzmann, Norman. 1991. A General Problem of Creation: Why Would God Create Anything at All? In *Being and Goodness: The Concept of the Good in Metaphysics and Philosophical Theology*, ed. Scott MacDonald, 208–228. Ithaca: Cornell University Press.

Kronen, John, and Eric Reitan. 2011. *God's Final Victory*. New York: Bloomsbury Publishing.

Kvanvig, Jonathan. 1993. *The Problem of Hell*. New York: Oxford University Press.

Langtry, B. 2008. *God, the Best, and Evil*. Oxford: Oxford University Press.

Larrimore, Mark, ed. 2001. *The Problem of Evil*. Malden: Blackwell Publishing.

Leftow, Brian. 2011. Why Perfect Being Theology? *International Journal for Philosophy of Religion* 69: 103–118.

———. 2012. *God and Necessity*. Oxford: Oxford University Press.

Leibniz, Gottfried Wilhelm. 1996. Essays on the Justice of God and the Freedom of Man. In *Theodicy*, ed. Austin Farrer and trans. E. M. Huggard. Chicago: Open Court.

Lepp, Ignace. 1964. *The Ways of Friendship*. New York: Macmillan Company.

Lewis, C.S. 1946. *The Great Divorce*. London: C.S. Lewis Pte. Ltd.

———. 2001. (orig. 1940). *The Problem of Pain*. New York: HarperOne

Lewis, David. 2000. Evil for Freedom's Sake. In *Papers in Ethics and Social Philosophy*, ed. Davis Lewis. Cambridge: Cambridge University Press.

Lim, Daniel. 2017. Doing Allowing and the Problem of Evil. *International Journal for Philosophy of Religion* 81: 273–289.

Lloyd-Jones, Martyn. 2001. *Why Does God Allow War?* Wheaton: Crossway Books.

Mackie, J.L. 1955. Evil and Omnipotence. *Mind* 64: 200–212.

Madden, Edward, and Peter Hare. 1968. *Evil and the Concept of God*. Springfield: Charles C. Thomas Publisher.

Maitzen, Stephen. 2009. Skeptical Theism and Moral Obligation. *International Journal for Philosophy of Religion* 65: 93–103.

Maritain, Jacques. 1942a. *St. Thomas and the Problem of Evil*. Milwaukee: Marquette University Press.

———. 1942b. *God and the Permission of Evil*. Trans. Joseph Evans. Milwaukee: Bruce.

McBrayer, Justin. 2010. Skeptical Theism. *Philosophical Compass* 5/7: 611–623.

McBrayer, Justin, and Daniel Howard-Snyder, eds. 2013. *Blackwell Companion to the Problem of Evil*. Malden: John Wiley and Sons.

McCabe, Herbert. 2010. *God and Evil in the Theology of Thomas Aquinas*. New York: Continuum International Publishing Group.

McCann, H. 2005. The Author of Sin? *Faith and Philosophy* 22: 144–159.

———. 2009. Pointless Suffering: How to Make the Problem of Evil Sufficiently Serious. In *Oxford Studies in Philosophy of Religion*, ed. J. Kvanvig, 2. Oxford: Oxford University Press.

McDonald, H.D. 1935. *The Atonement of the Death of Christ*. Grand Rapids: Baker Book House.

Meister, Chad. 2014. *Philosophy of Religion*. New York: Palgrave Macmillan.

———. 2018. *Evil a Guide to the Perplexed*. New York: Bloomsbury.

Meister, Chad, and James Dew, eds. 2017. *God and the Problem of Evil*. Downers Grove: InterVarsity Press.

Meister, Chad, and Paul Moser, eds. 2017. *The Cambridge Companion to the Problem of Evil*. Cambridge: Cambridge University Press.

Moon, Andrew. 2017. Plantinga's Religious Epistemology, Skeptical Theism, and Debunking Arguments. *Faith and Philosophy* 4: 449–470.

Morris, Thomas V. 1987. *Anselmian Explorations*. Notre Dame: University of Notre Dame Press.

Morris, Tom, and Matt Morris. 2005. *Superheroes and Philosophy: Truth, Justice and the Socratic Way*. Peru: Open Court.

Morton, Adam. 2004. *On Evil*. New York: Routledge.

Murphy, Mark C. 1998. Divine Command, Divine Will, and Moral Obligation. *Faith and Philosophy* 15: 3–27.

——— 2009. Morality and Divine Authority. In *The Oxford Handbook of Philosophical Theology*, ed. Thomas P. Flint and Michael Rea, 306–331. Oxford: Oxford University Press.

———. 2011. God Beyond Justice. In *Divine Evil? The Moral Character of the God of Abraham*, ed. Michael Bergmann, Michael Murray and Michael Rea. Oxford: Oxford University Press.

———. 2013. Perfect Goodness. *Stanford Encyclopedia of Philosophy*, ed. E.N. Zalta. http://plato.stanford.edu/entries/perfect-goodness/

Murphy, Mark. 2016. *God's Ethics*. New York: Oxford University Press.

Murray, M. 2008. *Nature Red in Tooth and Claw*. Oxford: Oxford University Press.

Neiman, Susan. 2015. *Evil in Modern Thought*. Princeton: Princeton University Press.

O'Neill, Onora. 2002. *Autonomy and Trust in Bioethics*. Cambridge: Cambridge University Press.

Oropeza, B.J. 2008. *The Gospel According to Superheroes*. New York: Peter Lang.

Parsons, Keith. 1989. *God and the Burden of Proof*. Amherst: Prometheus Books.

Peterson, Michael. 1982. *Evil and the Christian God*. Grand Rapids: Baker Book House.

———. 1998. *God and Evil*. Boulder: Westview Press.

Petrik, James. 2000. *Evil Beyond Belief*. Armonk: M.E. Sharpe.

Philips, D.Z. 2005. *The Problem of Evil and the Problem of God*. Minneapolis: Fortress Press.

Plaisted, Dennis. 2017. On Justifying One's Acceptance of Divine Command Theory. *International Journal for Philosophy of Religion* 81: 315–334.

Plantinga, Alvin. 1998. Degenerate Evidence and Rowe's New Evidential Argument from Evil. *Nous* 32: 531–544.

———. 2000. *Warranted Christian Belief*. Oxford: Oxford University Press.

Plantinga, Alvin, and Michael Tooley. 2008. *Knowledge of God*. Malden: Blackwell Publishing.

Pruss, Alexander. 2012. A Counterexample to Plantinga's Free Will Defense. *Faith and Philosophy* 29: 400–415.

Pryor, J. 2000. The Sceptic and the Dogmatist. *Nous* 34: 517–549.

Rea, Michael, ed. 2015. *Evil and the Hiddenness of God*. Stamford: Cengage Learning.

———. 2018. *Divine Hiddenness*. Oxford: Oxford University Press.

Reichenbach, Bruce. 1982. *Evil and a Good God*. New York: Fordham University Press.

Rhoda, Alan. 2010. Gratuitous Evil and Divine Providence. *Religious Studies*. 46: 281–302.

Rogers, Katherin. 2000. *Perfect Being Theology*. Edinburgh: University of Edinburgh Press.

Rorty, Amelie. 2001. *The Many Faces of Evil*. New York: Routledge.

Routley, R. 1979. Against the Inevitability of Human Chauvinism. In *Ethics and Problems of the 21st Century*, ed. K.E. Goodpaster and K.M. Sayre. Notre Dame: University of Notre Dame Press.

Rowe, William. 1996. The Evidential Argument from Evil: A Second Look. In *The Evidential Argument from Evil*, ed. D. Howard-Snyder, 262–285. Bloomington: Indiana University Press.

———. 1998. Reply to Plantinga. *Nous* 32: 545–551.

———. 2001a. Skeptical Theism: A Response to Bergmann. *Nous* 35: 297–303.

———, ed. 2001b. *God and the Problem of Evil*. Malden: Blackwell Publishing.

———. 2005. *Can God Be Free?* New York: Oxford University Press.

Russell, Luke. 2014. *Evil: A Philosophical Investigation*. New York: Oxford University Press.

Rutledge, Jonathan. 2017. Skeptical Theism, Moral Skepticism, and Epistemic Propriety. *International Journal for Philosophy of Religion* 8: 263–272.

Schulwets, Harold. 1983. *Evil and the Morality of God*. Cincinnati: Hebrew Union College Press.

Sehon, S. 2010. The Problem of Evil: Skeptical Theism Leads to Moral Paralysis. *International Journal for Philosophy of Religion* 67: 67–80.

Seifert, Josef. 2016. *Where Was God in Auschwitz?* Granada: International Academy of Philosophy Press.

Smith, George. 1979. *Atheism the Case Against God*. Buffalo: Prometheus Press.

Southgate, Christopher. 2008. *The Groaning of Creation*. Louisville: Westminster John Knox Press.

Sovik, Atle. 2011. *The Problem of Evil and the Power of God*. Leiden: Brill.

Speak, Daniel. 2015a. *The Problem of Evil*. Malden: Polity Press.

———. 2015b. Domination and the Free Will Defense: A Reply to Pruss. *Faith and Philosophy* 3: 313–324.

Stenger, Victor. 2007. *God: The Failed Hypothesis*. Amherst: Prometheus.

Stump, Eleanore. 2010. *Wandering in the Darkness: Narrative and the Problem of Suffering*. Oxford: Oxford University Press.

———. 2018. *Atonement*. New York: Oxford University Press.

Svendsen, Lars. 2010. *A Philosophy of Evil*. Champaign: Dalkey Archive Press.

Swedenborg, Emanuel. 2007. *Divine Providence*. Trans. William Wunsch. Radford: A & D Publishing.

Swinburne, Richard 1991. *The Existence of God*. Revised ed. Oxford: Clarendon Press.

———. 1993. *The Coherence of Theism*. Revised ed. Oxford: Oxford University Press.

———. 2004. *The Existence of God*. 2nd ed. Oxford: Oxford University Press.

Talbott, Thomas. 1999. *The Inescapable Love of God*. Parkland: Universal Publishers.

Taylor, Paul. 1987. *Respect for Nature*. Princeton: Princeton University Press.

Tomberlin, James, and Peter van Inwagen. 1985. *Alvin Plantinga*. Dordrecht: D. Reidel.

Tooley, Michael. 2002 (revised 2009). The Problem of Evil. In *The Stanford Encyclopedia of Philosophy*, ed. E.N. Zalta. http://plato.stanford.edu/archives/spr2010/entries/evil/

Tooley, Michael, and Alvin Plantinga. 2008. *Knowledge of God*. Oxford: Blackwell.

Trakakis, N. 2007. *The God Beyond Belief: In Defense of William Rowe's Evidential Argument from Evil.* Dordrecht: Springer Publishing.

Tweedt, Chris. 2015. Defusing the Common Sense Problem of Evil. *Faith and Philosophy* 4: 391–403.

van Inwagen, P. 1988. The Magnitude, Duration, and Distribution of Evil: A Theodicy. *Philosophical Topics* 16: 161–187.

———. 1991. The Problem of Evil, the Problem of Air, and the Problem of Silence. *Philosophical Perspectives* 5: 135–165.

———., ed. 2004. *Christian Faith and the Problem of Evil.* Grand Rapids: Eerdmans.

Varner, Gary. 1998. *In Nature's Interests?* New York: Oxford University Press.

Viney, Donald. 1985. *Charles Hartshorne and the Existence of God.* Albany: State University of New York Press.

Wall, Jerry. 2002. *Heaven: The Logic of Eternal Joy.* New York: Oxford University Press.

Walvoord, John. 1996. *Four Views of Hell.* Grand Rapids: Zondervan.

Warmke, Brandon. 2017. God's Standing to Forgive. *Faith and Philosophy* 34: 381–402.

Whitehead, Alfred. 1926. *Religion in the Making.* New York: Macmillan.

Wielenberg, Erik. 2004. A Morally Unsurpassable God Must Create the Best. *Religious Studies* 40: 43–62.

———. 2008. *God and the Reach of Reason.* Cambridge: Cambridge University Press.

———. 2010. Skeptical Theism and Divine Lies. *Religious Studies* 46: 509–523.

Wiesel, Elie. 1985. *Night.* Trans. Marion Wiesel. New York: Hill and Wang.

———. 1995. *The Trial of God.* Trans. Marion Wiesel. New York: Schocken Books.

Wiley, Tatha. 2002. *Original Sin.* Mahwah: The Paulist Press.

William of Ockham. 1979. On the Four Books of Sentences. In *Divine Command Morality*, ed. Janice Idziak. New York: Edwin Mellon Press.

Williams, Bernard, and J.J.C. Smart. 1973. *Utilitarianism: For and Against.* Cambridge: Cambridge University Press.

Wykstra, S. 1996. Rowe's Noseeum Arguments from Evil. In *The Evidential Argument from Evil*, ed. D. Howard-Snyder, 126–150. Bloomington: Indiana University Press.

———. 2007. CORNEA, Carnap, and Current Closure Befuddlement. *Faith and Philosophy* 24: 87–98.

Wynn, Mark. 1999. *God and Goodness.* New York: Routledge.

Index[1]

A

Absolute deontologist, 45n1,
    101n25, 137–138n17
Adams, Marilyn, 8n9, 14, 37–42,
    47n11, 47n12, 47n13,
    48n16, 99n12, 170
Aliens, 58, 158, 159
Alternative understandings of
    significant freedom, 12
    Plantinga's understanding, 12
Angelou, Mayo, 68n15
Aquinas, Thomas, 2, 44, 68n16,
    111, 112, 119, 123, 124,
    134, 135, 183

Aristotle, 112, 119
Atheists, 1, 7, 7n2, 52, 60,
    100n24, 115, 124,
    126–129, 131,
    181, 183, 189, 191
Auschwitz, 174

B

Beatific vision, 36, 46n6, 104n48
Bergmann, Michael, vi, 71–78,
    82, 85, 92–96, 98n11,
    100n24, 108n67
Best possible world, 191

---

[1] Note: Page numbers followed by 'n' refer to notes.

© The Author(s) 2019
J. P. Sterba, *Is a Good God Logically Possible?*,
https://doi.org/10.1007/978-3-030-05469-4

Greater good justification, 26,
124, 125, 130
Greater Moral Good Defense, 30

H

Harm in a broader sense to include
offense, 154n9
Hartshorne, Charles, 192
Heavenly afterlife, 36–38, 40–43,
45n2, 45n3, 46–47n7,
47n10, 47n13, 48n15, 53,
58, 65, 66, 68n12, 82, 83,
88, 93, 95, 103n42,
105n48, 107n63
Hick, John, 170, 171
Horrendous evil, 2, 7n1, 14, 22, 26,
43, 47n13, 52, 53, 58, 63,
67n3, 67n6, 68n15, 73–75,
78–80, 82–89, 92–97,
102n35, 103n39, 103n43,
104n47, 105n48, 105n50,
106n53, 108n65, 117, 122,
124–131, 133, 135,
138n29, 145, 149–153,
155n15, 155n21, 159,
160, 164–166, 173, 175,
176, 177n9, 182,
184–187, 189, 190,
192, 193n4, 193n8
definition of, 14, 193n8

I

Ichneumonidae, 157, 158, 160,
168, 176n1, 176n2,
178n16, 193n3
Inner acts, 121, 122

I

Intended, 7n3, 7n4, 8n8, 12,
13, 21, 22, 31n2, 51,
53–55, 67n3, 67n4,
75, 81, 121, 123,
125, 131, 132, 161,
179n23, 181

J

Jesus Christ, 37, 43, 74, 99n16,
102–103n39, 141,
143–145, 150, 151,
154n4, 177n12
Just political state
an ideally just and powerful
political state
the analogy of, 6, 32n17, 56,
69n23, 152, 153, 161, 173,
182, 190, 191

L

Lewis, C.S., 172
Lewis, David, 52
Libertarians, 15–18, 27, 31n6
Limited intervention, 60, 62, 63,
132–134, 174

M

Mackie, John, 1, 7n2, 25, 26,
136n5, 136n7, 155n22,
182, 189, 190
Malum culpae, 119
Malum poenae, 119
Messiah, 141, 144, 151, 154n4
Metropolis, 64
Minority Report, 55

CPSIA information can be obtained
at www.ICGtesting.com
Printed in the USA
LVHW050759070819
626826LV00012B/258